MW00930432

PRAISE FOR LIFE IN THE FAITH LANE

Have you ever felt stuck in your spiritual journey? Bea Sprouse's new book, *Life in the Faith Lane*, provides a thought-provoking perspective on living a life of faith. Full of practical guidance and personal insights, this book will inspire you to pursue a deeper relationship with God and help you find purpose and fulfillment in life.

– Craig Groeschel
Founding Pastor of Life.Church and
New York Times Best-Selling Author

This book will challenge you to answer the question that Jesus posed in Luke 18:8. Will He find faith on the earth when He returns? You too can throw off the traditions of men and live a world-changing life in the faith lane.

– Dr. John Benefiel
Founding Pastor of Church on the Rock, Oklahoma City
Founding Apostle of the Heartland Apostolic Prayer Network

The anointed pages of this captivating title exceed all expectations. Ken and Bea Sprouse trusted God and pleased Him. Like the Apostle Paul, they lived by the faith of the Son of God and Christ lived in them. God's astonishing grace is interwoven throughout their experiences. The reader will instantly feel a sense of belonging to this precious, flourishing family because they are a microcosm of God's household. Moreover, one will be drawn closer to God. Ken is still alive in the Spirit, and Mike and Bea Sprouse are an epistle of Christ radiantly blessing the lives of others. The just shall live by faith.

– Pastor Carolyn P. Bynum
Restoration Christian Ministries, Sierra Vista, AZ

~

It would be difficult to find someone who speaks the truth and walks in love as much as Bea Sprouse. Her faith and love for Jesus are her lasting legacy, but the blessings that she pours out to everyone around her is how worlds change. The blessings and wisdom in these pages are priceless!

– Damian Wilson
Mechanical Engineer, Boeing

~

Bea has a story to tell, and she does it quite well. A delightful read!

– Dr. Phil Chandler
Retired Director, OSU-OKC

~

I have known Bea as a person who knows how to draw people, gather them, and empower them. It is an honor, forty-five years later, to still call her friend and sister in the Lord.

I know you will be blessed and encouraged as you read her story. I love the title of her book. I can testify that I have watched her live it. It is an honor for me to have been a part of it.

– Rickey Musgrove
Pastor, God's Light Shining, Edmond, OK

~

After teaching in Madras in 1996, we could see that Ken and Bea were two of the best instructors we have had at Faith Tech Ministries. Their teaching skills and love for people shine through. People will be blessed and inspired as they read this book.

– Bob and Karen Reid
Founders and Directors, Faith Tech

~

Bea Sprouse tells a beautiful story of life, love, and God's faithfulness throughout the years in *Life in the Faith Lane*. Reading Bea's book will inspire you to love more deeply, trust more openly, and live life as one who is dearly loved and cherished by God.

– Kelly Osborne
Executive Minister, The Springs Church of Christ

Bea's decades of living, expressing and modeling scripturally based love, grace, mercy, character and God directed decision making processes have steered countless wanderers onto or back onto the Lord's FULFILLING, yet straight and narrow path to live on purpose, the full and abundant life He offers us all. We choose to receive, Lord. Yes indeed, *Life in the Faith Lane* will bless and encourage you. Our Lord God is faithful — Yesterday, Now and Always!

– May Ellen, Milton and Fran Rathbun
Bea's Loving Siblings

∾

If you're familiar with the phrase, "walk the walk," you're probably acquainted with Bea Sprouse. Over 38 years of walking with her have proven that she is the real deal. You will do well to absorb the wisdom you find in this book.

– Maurice and Connie Golden
Beloved In-Laws

∾

Having known Bea Sprouse for almost 40 years now, I can assure anyone reading this book that the title *Life in the Faith Lane* is most apropos. It describes every aspect of her life. She never swerves out of that lane. There may be moments that she slows down, but only to help those who may be struggling to stay within the lines of their own faith lane. True to her family, true to her friends, true to her convictions and most importantly true to her faith in her good and wonderful Savior. So, on your mark, get set, go. Join

Bea as she describes her incredible journey in *Life in the Faith Lane*.

– Taunya McCarty
Teacher, God's Light Shining

～

Buckle up and enjoy the ride as you journey through Bea's life, from pitfalls to prosperity, and see the hand of the Father woven through the BEAutiful tapestry of it all.

– Stacy Sarkey Rosete
Edmond Christian Center Worship Team

～

Life in the Faith Lane will truly bless you and encourage you to go beyond what you think you can accomplish in a faith walk with Christ.

– Howard and Deanna Rogers
Deacon, Lonestar Baptist Church

～

It's my great pleasure to authenticate this book called *Life in the Faith* Lane written by Bea Sprouse.

She has been my spiritual mentor and guide since 1996 when she first came to India. She is a lady of faith and great integrity. She has been a source of inspiration and blessing, a very God-fearing person, well-rooted in the faith of our Lord and Savior Jesus Christ. I know her personally as a very spiritual person, and she lives a triumphant life.

This book will encourage all the readers and help them to cope with all the ups and downs of life. I very strongly recommend this book to one and all, as I am sure many will benefit from it.

— **Pastors John & Shiny Jackson**
India

∼

As a pastor in India, I can say that Bea Sprouse has never tired of traveling here to help. She and Ken were our first real teachers, among many others. They taught us the Word of God and brought us Bibles, notebooks, pens and study kits. Even after Ken went to heaven, Bea continued the work here. We call India Bea's second home. We've witnessed her encounter and overcome many obstacles. I know this book will bless every reader.

— **Pastor Moorthi**
India

∼

Bea is the epitome of a Proverbs 31 woman, which is one of my great aspirations in life. She is a woman of many gifts and talents, and she seems to have boundless energy. Bea has a flair for life which has led her on many adventures. I am amazed at all the different places she has traveled and the things she has accomplished! She has lived a life to be admired, and this memoir will be a treasure added to any library!

– Cher Gromer Hampton
Former Student, God's Light Shining

~

I have known Bea for 26 years, and one of the things that has always stood out to me is her faith. I have watched in amazement and awe as she has maneuvered through life with a faith that is exorbitant. Her deep love for Jesus shows in her faith walk. She is a leader and example in this area. One we can all look to her and say, "I want that kind of faith."

– Pattsi Thornbrue
ECA Parent

~

I have watched Bea live her *Life in the Faith Lane* for over fifty years. We began our friendship teaching at the OKC Adult Education Center together. We immediately knew that our lives would forever be entwined. Our first babies were born seven weeks apart, and we have had an everlasting bond ever since. I can say with certainty that Bea has never veered from that lane of complete devotion to the Lord and that she has committed her life to serving Him. I'm forever grateful for her presence in my heart and life.

– Pam Holbrook
Retired Oklahoma City Public School Teacher

~

I have observed Bea's Christian example through sixty years of friendship. She not only talks the talk, but truly walks the walk. Bea has continued to be a Godly woman who invests her time and talents to God's glory. Thank you, Bea. Observing your journey with the Lord has truly been an inspiration and honor not only for me but many others! *"I thank my God upon every remembrance of you."* Philippians 1:3

– Connie Matney Jones
Pastor's Daughter, Corum Baptist Church

~

Like me, readers will be lifted and encouraged by Bea's lifetime of walking in faith, as only she can tell it.

– Stephanie West
ARTS, Dance Assistant

~

Having known Bea Sprouse for over four decades, I have always been *so* proud of her many accomplishments that she has accomplished for Christ. As a family, they seek first the Kingdom as they make the Word of God first and final authority in their lives. Follow her example in *Life in the Faith Lane* as she follows Christ.

– Linda Weaver
Word of Life Center Teacher

Bea improved the quality of life for those around her, while being an example of a Proverbs 31 wife and friend. 'To know Bea is to love her' would be a fitting accolade. Reading her memoir will be like experiencing the Bible in our modern world. It is a journey to eternity. The reader will be blessed as Bea shares her pilgrimage.

– Hilliard Shackford
Okie Smoker/Fellow Faith Walker

Bea Sprouse is a strong woman of faith. I've observed her struggle through challenges and overcome them. She doesn't just talk the religious lingo but loves God wholeheartedly and trusts Him with everything in her blessed life. Anything she has to say is definitely worth hearing.

– Debbie Morris
Administrative Assistant, Edmond Christian Academy

"I have known and worked with Bea for over 50 years. She is a God-loving, God-sharing Christian woman of many attributes. I wish her success in this, her current undertaking."

– Russell Kline
Retired Professor, OSU

Bea is among the most influential pillars of the faith in my life. She taught me to know, love and serve Jesus as a little girl. Bea continued to have a wonderful influence over my life through Edmond Christian Academy, the school she and Ken founded. As my English teacher, Bea often had us write scriptures to memorize, label and diagram to learn grammar. To this day I recite and sing scripture I learned as a child to do spiritual battle or praise Jesus. The precious memories I have of Bea and the impact she has had on my life stretch beyond anything I could write for the purposes of this book. I am grateful that I still have the privilege and honor to call her my friend after 35 years. She represents the face, voice, hands and feet of our Lord Jesus Christ. For that, I give God all the glory.

—Jennifer Rutledge Carney
Former Student, Edmond Christian Academy

LIFE IN THE FAITH LANE

Overcoming the Traditions of Men

BEA SPROUSE

with
MELANIE HEMRY

CONTENTS

Unless otherwise noted, scripture quotations from The Authorized (King James) Version. Rights in the Authorized Version in the United Kingdom are vested in the Crown. Reproduced by permission of the Crown's patentee, Cambridge University Press.

Scripture quotations marked NKJV are taken from the New King James Version. Copyright © 1979, 1980, 1982, Thomas Nelson, Inc.

Scripture quotations marked NASB are taken from the *New American Standard Bible*. Copyright © The Lockman Foundation 1960, 1962, 1963, 1968, 1971, 1972, 1973, 1975, 1977, 1995. Used by permission.

"Scripture quotations taken from the Amplified® Bible (AMP), Copyright © 2015 by The Lockman Foundation. Used by permission lockman.org" If from the 1987 edition (or earlier): "Scripture quotations taken from the Amplified® Bible (AMPC), Copyright © 1954, 1958, 1962, 1964, 1965, 1987 by The Lockman Foundation Used by permission. lockman.org"

Life in the Faith Lane: Overcoming the Traditions of Men

© Copyright 2023 by Bea Sprouse

Published by Writing Momentum LLC

Cover design by Hester Designs and Writing Momentum LLC

Print and ebook formatting by Writing Momentum LLC

Printed in the United States of America.

All rights reserved.

No part of this publication may be reproduced, stored in a retrieval system, or transmitted in any form or by any means—electronic, mechanical, photocopy, recording, or any other— except for brief quotations in reviews, without the prior permission of the publisher.

Chapter One

WHEN ONLY GOD CAN HELP

The Oklahoma sun hadn't gotten the memo that it was only May that morning in 1980. My husband, Ken, and I sweltered as we pounded the pavement during our five-mile run. After 14 years of marriage, I still enjoyed every moment I spent with him. Even running. There was something about matching our strides in that tedious, repetitive action that made the world around us fade away. I rubbed my hand over my bulging belly, just checking in with the baby.

We'd left from our front door in Edmond, Oklahoma, and were running a route through neighborhoods to Broadway Avenue before looping back. "Don't you have a doctor's appointment today?" he asked.

"Yes, today's my checkup. We've also got Mike and his parents coming to dinner this evening."

Our daughter, Kendra Bea, whom we called Kendi, was almost eight, and I was seven months pregnant with our second child. When I was carrying Kendi, Ken's Aunt Lucy encouraged me to walk during my pregnancy to get in shape for a healthy delivery. Ken and I had walked every day, and I'd eaten a healthy diet. I felt better than I'd felt in my life. When I went into labor, I was admitted to Deaconess Hospital where they took me to X-ray. There were no sonograms back then, and they suspected that my baby was breach. Sure enough, she was.

Our two natural childbirth coaches stayed with me after their shift was over. Each time I had a contraction, they pushed because the baby couldn't. Three hours later, I delivered our first daughter.

In the years since her birth, Ken and I'd started running. I was now 33 and in great health. However, the day I realized that I was pregnant, I searched the scriptures to see what God had to say about having children. The Bible is full of God's promises regarding childbirth, and I wrote down scriptural confessions about our baby. Ken and I confessed them aloud several times a day during my pregnancy.

"I am redeemed from the curse put on Eve because of her sin. I do not have sorrow, pain or toil in childbirth because Jesus redeemed me from this curse (Genesis 3:16)."

Based on Exodus 23:25-26 I said, "He has taken sickness from me, and I shall not lose my baby, for He will fulfill my days."

I also made my own confessions that I spoke aloud every day. "We have a perfect, healthy, normal baby," I said. "I have a perfect pregnancy. I will have a perfect, short, fast, painless delivery with no complications. The baby is in the proper position and will come out headfirst, face down, rotating the correct way. I speak Jesus' healing and creative power over my placenta."

LIVING IN THE FAST LANE

Ken had left his job as a school counselor to work full-time in the restaurant industry. I worked as a professor at the Oklahoma City campus of Oklahoma State University. At different times over the years, we served as church youth leaders, children's pastors and cell group leaders. We opened and ran 87 restaurants, cooked and entertained at home, counseled both students and adults, and traveled.

We'd planned our lives so that we could maximize our time together. If Ken had a project, I was involved. If I had a project, he was there as well. Somehow, we always lived life in the fast lane, enjoying every moment of the experience. But even by our standards, life had been more hectic than usual. Ken's dad had died, and I'd been helping his mother pack up her home of 40 years in Walters, Oklahoma to move to Oklahoma City. Our running was a short respite from our hectic schedule, good for both body and soul.

Later that day, I left my office and drove to the appointment with my doctor. As he examined my sonogram, he frowned and furrowed his brows.

"Your baby isn't growing." He stared with deep concentration at the screen.

"You have a detached placenta," he said finally.

"What do you mean?"

"That's why your baby's not growing. The baby's not getting any nourishment from your body. This is very dangerous for both of you." He sighed, rubbing his face and taking a deep breath, gathering himself to deliver the terrible news. "I honestly don't know if your baby will make it. This pregnancy is *very high risk.* Don't go back to work. You'll need to spend the rest of your pregnancy in bed."

I felt like I'd stumbled into a match with Muhammad Ali and been knocked out of the ring. I left the office reeling.

TAKING A STAND

I called Ken and told him what the doctor had said. He paused before he spoke, choosing each word with careful precision. We understood what the Bible says about the power of our words. What the doctor said about the situation was less important than what God said. As the parents of this child and God's representatives on earth, we knew that heaven and hell were listening for us to say what would happen next. What we said—or didn't say—would set the course for this child's life.

I sensed the Holy Spirit nudging a reminder that we should *choose life*—a reference to Deuteronomy 30:19. "This day I call the heavens and the earth as witnesses against you that I have set before you life and death, blessings and curses. Now *choose life*, so that you and your children may live" (emphasis mine).

The other scriptural admonition echoing in my mind was, *Death and life are in the power of the tongue.* The entire verse says, "Death and life are in the power of the tongue, And those who love it *and* indulge it will eat its fruit *and* bear the consequences of their words" (Proverbs 18:21 AMP).

In other words, there would be consequences—good or bad; life or death—based on our words and our response to this situation. What I *felt* like doing, and what I would have done before I learned those biblical truths, was call my family and friends weeping as I told them that my placenta had detached. I would have curled up in bed and put the news out as a prayer request to the whole church. They would have mobilized a team of volunteers to bring food, clean and help take care of Kendi.

But we both knew too much about how the Kingdom of God operated to do that. Ken and I understood that we couldn't afford to give in to our emotions. We couldn't afford to talk about what *might* happen.

GUARDING OUR WORDS

There were a thousand unspoken words between us. Kendi and this new baby were the most important people in our world. We could not allow ourselves even to imagine losing one of them, let alone speak of it.

"It won't hurt to rest," Ken said, his words measured and guarded. "Go to work and tell them you need a few days off. Then we'll pray."

I drove back to OSU and explained to my boss that I needed to take a few days off. A former registered nurse, she raised an eyebrow. "You all right?"

"I'm great," I said, waving goodbye as I left her office.

I drove home in a daze, my mind flitting around like a bird with no perch to land on. I thought back to the days of my childhood, growing up in the pews of Corum Baptist Church. I loved that church almost as much as my parents' 80-acre centennial farm on Beaver Creek near Corum, Oklahoma. It was there that I first learned about the goodness of God and His incredible love. I gave my heart and life to Jesus there, praying for my future husband.

The devil has given the Church a substitute for faith; one that looks and sounds so much like faith that few people can tell the difference. The substitute is called mental assent. Many people agree that the Bible is true, but they are only agreeing with their minds. That is mental assent, and it's not what gets the job done. It takes heart faith to receive from God.

—JOHN WESLEY

MAKING GOD'S WORD FINAL

Ken and I attended the Baptist Church as adults, involving ourselves in everything. Something changed in 1975 when we attended an evening Bible study. The handout that went with the lesson had a little questionnaire. One of the questions asked why we'd come to Bible study that night. Afterwards, Ken and I compared our answers. We'd both answered that we came out of a sense of duty.

We'd looked at one another in shock. What had happened to us? How had we gotten to a place of serving God out of duty instead of the fresh fires of love? Was this all there was? A life of duty? We discussed it in depth and prayed about it together.

We agreed that something was very wrong with our spiritual lives.

After a great deal of soul searching and prayer, we took a giant, dramatic step.

We committed to one another and to God, that from that day forward, we would no longer live by any church doctrines. We wouldn't live by our traditions. *In a radical move, we decided that we would live our lives as though every word of the Bible was true.*

Either God was a liar, or He wasn't.

We believed the Bible was true.

We would do what it said. Period. We would believe it. In the most literal sense.

And we would act on it.

It didn't sound radical—until you stepped off the deep end of the ocean and lived your life as though it was true. Only then did we realize how seldom most people do. It was only after we took that radical step that we began to realize how steeped in traditions we and most other Christians we knew were.

John Wesley once said, "The devil has given the Church a substitute for faith; one that looks and sounds so much like faith that few people can tell the difference. The substitute is called mental assent. Many people agree that the Bible is true, but they are only agreeing with their minds. That is mental assent, and it's not what gets the job done. It takes heart faith to receive from God."

What only amounts to about 12 inches—the distance from your head to your heart—turns out to be a million-mile, life-long sojourn.

Sometime later, Ken and I developed a code word we whispered to each other when we notice this substitute faith trying to creep back into our lives. *Counterfeit.*

A DRAMATIC DECISION

Somehow, we needed to learn how to move our faith from our heads to our hearts. Mental assent, we realized, would wear us out. It made life in Christ something to check off a list. We wanted the kind of Christian life we read about in the Bible. That same life-changing, world-transforming kind of faith that Peter, Paul and John lived. We didn't want to make excuses for why God didn't answer our prayers. We wanted a life in Christ that yielded results.

Now, we found ourselves facing *this*. It was one thing to step out on faith and act on God's Word for ourselves. But what were we willing to risk?

Our child?

Back home, I curled up on the sofa and opened my Bible. One thing we would *not* do was ask God to heal our baby and reattach the placenta *if it was His will*. That misuse of scripture had caused many a prayer to drop powerless to the ground.

The only place in Scripture that Jesus prayed those words was in the Garden of Gethsemane. Somehow, someone at some time tacked those same words onto a prayer for healing. It sounded so… *spiritual*.

What nobody ever seemed to notice was that Jesus never once used that phrase about healing—or about anything else. Neither did Paul, Peter, John, Mark or Matthew. None of the apostles, prophets or disciples prayed for healing *if it was God's will*.

Not once.

PRAYER OF CONSECRATION

That prayer, asking for God's will, which Jesus prayed in the Garden of Gethsemane, is a prayer of consecration. It's to be used when God's specific will isn't known. It was perfect when used to ask if there was a way to bypass the cross. Or if you didn't know who to marry, what job to take or where to live. It's for things that aren't in the Bible.

The reason it doesn't apply to healing is that God's will for healing is illustrated with clarity throughout the entire Bible. The Scripture leaves no wiggle room about God's will to heal. There was never a time in Scripture when Jesus refused to heal someone. Just the opposite. There are 101 things God said about healing in the Bible, and all of them confirm that it is His will to heal.

In Acts 10:38 the Bible says, "*even* Jesus of Nazareth, how God anointed him with the Holy Spirit and with power: who went about doing good, and *healing all* that were oppressed of the devil; for God was with him (ASV, emphasis mine).

Not only did Jesus go around healing the sick, He instructed His disciples, "Heal the sick, raise the dead, cleanse the lepers, cast out demons: freely ye received, freely give" (Matthew 10:8, ASV).

In Luke 10:9, Jesus said, "Heal the sick who are there and tell them, 'The kingdom of God has come near to you.'" This verse makes it clear that healing the sick was a sign of the kingdom of God!

I suggest that if you take the Bible at face value, you'll realize that it requires your own imagination to come up with reasons why God *might not heal.* What the Bible states is example after example of when God *does* heal.

JESUS PAID THE PRICE

How can we know for certain that healing is such an important aspect of God's plan for our lives? Because God includes it as part of our atonement on Calvary. In the Old Testament, the Prophet Isaiah, looking forward to Christ said, "But he was wounded for our transgressions, he was bruised for our iniquities: the chastisement of our peace was upon him; and with his stripes we are healed" (Isaiah 53:5, ASV).

When Matthew is giving his account of Jesus, he refers specifically to this passage: "When evening came, many who were demon-possessed were brought to him, and he drove out the spirits with a word *and healed all the sick. This was to fulfill what was spoken through the prophet Isaiah:* "He took up our infirmities and bore our diseases" (Matthew 8:16-17, emphasis mine).

If that weren't clear enough, I Peter 2:24 makes it even more plain by referring to Calvary in the past tense. "…who Himself bore our sins in His own body on the tree, that we, having died to sins, might live for righteousness—*by whose stripes you were healed*" (NKJV, emphasis mine).

My emotions were still reeling from the doctor's words, but as I read and reread these scriptures, I found a measure of peace. The issue of healing was settled in the Bible. In the hearts and minds of most Christians, not so much.

I looked up as Ken stepped through the door, grateful that he'd left work early to be with me. Striding to the sofa, he gathered me into his arms. "Everything's going to be all right," he said. His quiet assurance in God settled over me like a soft blanket.

We didn't waste time discussing what might or might not happen. We both understood that from this moment forward, our tongues would be under tighter control than ever before.

"God is so good," Ken sang as he pressed a hand over my protruding belly. *"God is so good, He's so good to me."* We both sang praises to God, giving Him glory for all the wonderful things He'd done for us. We rehearsed past victories, thanking Him for His faithfulness. We worshipped Him from our hearts, thanking Him for Kendi. We thanked Him for this baby and what a wonderful gift she was to us already. We praised God until His presence permeated the room.

MOUNTAIN MOVING FAITH

We knew God's Word was bigger and more powerful than any words spoken by men. Our confidence was in who God says He is, not in the report of a doctor.

Turning to Mark 11:22-23, Ken read, "Truly I tell you, if anyone says to this mountain, 'Go, throw yourself into the sea,' and does not doubt in their heart but believes that what they say will happen, it will be done for them. Therefore I tell you, whatever you ask for in prayer, believe that you have received it, and it will be yours."

Ken called our pastors, Rickey and Karla Musgrove, and asked them to come to our house. Early that evening, before Ken's cousin Mike Sprouse and his parents arrived, Rickey and Karla came over. We discussed the doctor's report with them. They prayed and agreed with us that God Himself would reattach the placenta and that our baby would be born on time and healthy.

Ken and I followed the example of Galatians 1:15-16: "But when it pleased God, who separated me from my mother's womb, and called me by his grace, to reveal his Son in me, that I might preach him among the heathen; immediately I conferred not with flesh and blood."

We didn't confer with flesh and blood either. We told no one else. We weren't going to risk anyone else's negative confessions of doubt and unbelief.

This became our habit. We took our requests to God, not man. We began making the Word of God our first and final authority in every area of our lives. As we continued our spiritual journey, we found a remnant who believed the Word as we did.

If we shared any prayer requests, it was to those of like-minded faith. Sadly, many well-meaning Christians don't know how to stand on God's Word with you in prayer. Hebrews 4:16 says, "Let us then approach God's throne of grace with confidence, so that we may receive mercy and find grace to help us in our time of need." Some prayer meetings turn into gossip sessions, never making it to the throne room.

Chapter Two

RESTING IN GOD'S WORD

I sorted through the notes on my podium as college students shuffled into class, laughing and talking. Books dropped onto desktops and book bags sagged to the floor. I breathed the scent of chalk from the assignments I'd written on the blackboard.

It was good to be back at work.

One week after being told that my baby's placenta had detached, and our taking our place in prayer, I had returned to work. I'd also returned to our full schedule of activities, including our morning runs.

Believing and acting on God's Word was counterintuitive to the way most Christians lived. It was counterintuitive to the way Ken and I had lived before taking the radical step of trusting that God's Word was true.

The alternative, of course, was living by an idolatrous mix of the Bible and the traditions of men. Jesus wasn't thrilled with the Pharisees for living that way. I believe that it is those traditions that have robbed the church today of its miraculous power.

According to the Bible, the problem stemmed from believing and acting on traditions taught by men, which were not scriptural. Jesus accused the Pharisees of this in Mark 7:13. "Thus you are nullifying *and* making void *and* of no effect [the authority of] the Word of God through your tradition, which you [in turn] hand on. And many things of this kind you are doing" (AMP).

Traditions of men nullify the Gospel.

None of us wants to be pharisaical, but most all of us have been taught things as truth which oppose the written word of God. Regarding healing, the tradition of men, which is taught by most churches, is that if you pray and you don't see your answer manifest, it means that God chose not to heal you.

SEPARATING TRUTH FROM TRADITION

That teaching is a tradition of man. It doesn't exist anywhere in the Bible.

In fact, the opposite is true.

Although there are many more, I'll share two scriptures that directly contradict that teaching.

First John 5:14-15 says this:

> And this is the confidence (the assurance, the privilege of boldness) which we have in Him: [we are sure] that if we ask anything (make any request) according to His will (in agreement with His own plan), He listens to *and* hears us.

And if (since) we [positively] know that He listens to us in whatever we ask, we *also know [with settled and absolute knowledge] that we have [granted us as our present possessions]* the requests made of Him (AMP Classic, emphasis mine).

That's about as clear as it can get. I like this version of the Amplified Classic because it reminds us that we have our answer granted to us as our *present possession* when we pray.

Let's also look at Mark 11:23-24:

Verily I say unto you, Whosoever shall say unto this mountain, Be thou taken up and cast into the sea; and shall not doubt in his heart, but shall believe that what he saith cometh to pass; he shall have it. Therefore I say unto you, All things whatsoever ye pray and ask for, believe that ye receive them, and ye shall have them.

NOT BY SIGHT

True faith works this way: you must believe it *before* you see it. How long do you have to believe *without* seeing? I doubt you'll have to stand in faith as long as Abraham did, waiting for the fulfillment of his promised son.

That took 25 years, but according to the Bible, Abraham hoped in faith.

In other words, the traditions of man teach believers to live by sight. Like doubting Thomas. He said he wouldn't believe unless he could see the holes in Jesus' hands for himself.

The Bible teaches that we must live by faith and not by sight.

Ken and I were stunned when we realized how much of what we'd believed were actually just traditions of men. That's why we made a vow to God to take Him at His word. As soon as we prayed with Rickey and Karla that day, asking God to knit the baby's placenta back together, as far as we were concerned it was done. Finished.

The traditions of man teach, "Well, you never know what God's going to do. You'd better get in bed just to be safe."

What a lie. We knew just what God was going to do. He'd do what He said He would. Since we believed that God had already answered our prayer, and we had that placenta reattached as our present possession, there was no reason for me to stay in bed. There was no reason *not* to return to our normal, hectic life. There was no reason *not* to run.

My doctor assumed that I was on bedrest. When I went in for my appointments, I didn't see any reason to mention to him that I was back to life as normal. During one checkup he said, "What kind of anesthetic do you want?"

"I don't want any," I explained. "I want natural childbirth."

"But this is a *high-risk* pregnancy!" he snapped. "You *will* have an anesthetic!"

I didn't argue or contradict him. While he didn't realize it yet, I already knew that what happened would depend on what Ken and I were agreeing with God. We were in covenant with God, not the doctor.

We respected our doctor for his knowledge and experience, but our trust was in God, not medicine.

LIVING LIFE TO THE FULLEST

As the weeks passed, we continued living in a whirlwind of activity. In addition to everything else, I finished helping Ken's mother pack and get moved to Oklahoma City. I didn't fret about the baby; I had great peace and joy. Although sometimes during those long, tedious runs, my mind wandered to countless people who'd tried to take a major step of faith and fallen flat.

It happened often. When it did, people lost hope and believed that they couldn't take God at His Word on important issues like health, life and death. My heart went out to them because I knew the problem was a lack of knowledge. In Hosea 4:6 we're told, "My people are destroyed for lack of knowledge..." (NKJV).

 So then faith *comes* by hearing, and hearing by the word of God.

— ROMANS 10:17, NKJV

They weren't perishing for a lack of medical knowledge, although that could be true as well. Most of the time when we experience faith failures, it's because there are things about God's Word that we don't understand.

Misguided people who asked God to heal their vision and then threw away their glasses as an act of faith might be a good example. What had they missed in the Bible?

Romans 10:17 teaches us, "So then faith comes by hearing, and hearing by the word of God" (NKJV). Faith for a miracle doesn't come from throwing your glasses away. That's a misguided tradition of man. Faith comes by hearing, hearing and hearing more about what God says.

FAITH COMES BY HEARING

Of course, if you listen to God's message regarding salvation, over and over, that won't get you healed. For that, you need to hear God's specific words regarding healing. And you can't just hear them a few times and live off that revelation.

I like the way The Passion translates Romans 10:17, "Faith then, is birthed in a heart that responds to God's anointed utterance of the Anointed One." In other words, faith doesn't come from our head knowledge. True faith originates from a heart that has grasped the truth of God's will regarding healing, or whatever situation you face.

Since the day that Ken and I vowed to take God at His Word, we'd immersed ourselves in it. We read it. We confessed it. We meditated on it. We listened to anointed messages.

We kept our spiritual tanks filled with the Word of God. Now, when the enemy desired to kill our child, our faith tanks were not empty. They were full, and we continued hearing and hearing and hearing the Word of God regarding healing for our baby.

My due date, July 21, was fast approaching. Since I'd delivered Kendi well past my due date, I assumed that I would be late having this baby as well. We'd scheduled to leave that day to go to Tulsa for Kenneth Hagin's Camp Meeting.

RUNNING TOWARD THE GOAL

That morning, July 21, Ken and I went for our usual morning run. Afterwards we packed our bags and loaded the car. I felt great. Although I'd had a little bit of spotting here and there, I'd never had a contraction or suffered the false contractions known as Braxton Hicks. Yet, as we drove past Mercy Hospital on our way out of town, I heard myself say, "Maybe we should stop by and let them check me."

As soon as it came out of my mouth, I wondered why I'd said it.

Ken pulled in and parked. When a nurse examined me, she gasped. "You're about to have this baby!"

"She hasn't had a single labor pain," Ken insisted. "We only live four miles from here. Can we go home until she goes into labor?"

"Not unless you want to deliver this baby yourself at home!"

I was admitted and whisked to a labor room within minutes. The nurse flipped through my medical record. "You're supposed to have an anesthetic," she said.

"I know my doctor wrote that, but I really don't want one."

"Well," she said, pondering the situation, "the doctor isn't here, so I'll work with you until he arrives."

He didn't arrive in time.

Our daughter, Scotti, arrived so fast that there was no time or need for an anesthetic. Just as we'd prayed and confessed, I experienced a pain-free natural childbirth without complications. Although she was small, Scotti was healthy, perfect in every way.

The next morning, the doctor arrived to examine me. "I know you didn't do what I said, but you had a healthy baby and that's all that matters."

ONLY GOD

It's been over 40 years since God brought Scotti to us whole. While I carried her, I never looked up the dangers of a detached placenta. I knew that could knock me off my foundation of faith.

Some people may think that I risked my baby's life by not staying on bedrest. I don't agree. First, bedrest doesn't repair the damage. A placenta doesn't reattach itself. More important, there was no risk—unless God lied and His Word wasn't true.

He didn't, and it *is* true.

Even now, all these years later, there is still nothing you can do about a detached placenta. There are no medical miracles that allow a doctor to suture the placenta back where it belongs. Many children whose placentas detach still die. Others live but suffer cerebral palsy due to a lack of oxygen.

Repairing a detached placenta is still in the realm of a miracle from God. The One who knit Scotti in my womb, had no trouble knitting those tiny vessels back together and making sure she had all the oxygen and nutrition she needed.

Chapter Three

A HOLE IN THE HEART

*T*he sun sizzled, stinging the back of my neck and arms as I trudged down long rows of cotton fields on our family farm. Cotton hulls scratched my legs and poked holes in my fingers like thorns. The gunnysack slung over my shoulder was bigger than my six-year-old body.

I hated picking cotton. Back then, I didn't know that some kids didn't pull weeds, hoe the vegetable garden, gather eggs, milk cows or pick cotton. Life on our 80-acre farm wasn't full of fun and frolic. It was hard work—a family affair—all year long. But picking cotton was the worst.

Stumbling into the kitchen for lunch, tears made rivulets through the dirt on my face. "Mother," I cried holding up my bleeding finger, "see what happened?"

Mamma shoved me into the kitchen. "Go wash up." Stung, I looked at my brother and sisters. Why did she love them but not me? There were no lingering hugs or tender kisses. She never had time for me.

My mother didn't love me.

This was a fact of my life, just like chores on the farm. The pain and grief from that knowledge felt debilitating. I had a hole in my heart, a deep yearning to be loved by my mother. I knew Daddy loved me, but mother's affection was elusive and unattainable.

I don't know when I realized that she didn't love me. It might have been when I was two years old and my baby sister Fran was born premature, not expected to live. As an adult looking back, I have great compassion for my mother. I'm sure that she did love me, but as a child, I saw no sign of it. I never caught a hint of love's sweet scent.

I heard a minister say that God downloads our identity to us by the age of five. I believe that to be true. I know He did that for me. However, like anything precious to God, Satan sets out to steal it. For me, he stole my identity in the cruelest way possible. He convinced me that my mother didn't love me.

Your mother doesn't love you, he whispered in my ear. *There's something very wrong with you. You're unlovable.*

I lost myself in those lies. My wounded heart felt incomplete, unlovable. Wrong.

WOUNDED HEARTS

My father, an unshakable, kind, stable and loving man, married her when she was 16 and he was 29. I still have a black-and-white Kodak photograph of our family in those early days. At 20, Mother looked drawn, exhausted and far older than her age. My sister May was six years old. My brother Milton was five. I was two years old, and my baby sister Fran was a newborn.

As an adult, I can look at that picture and understand that Mother had more than her young emotions could handle. She was broken and wounded. As a child, I knew that she didn't have enough love to go around. There was none left for me.

My mother, Viola, was one of two children raised in a small, three-bedroom house in Walters, Oklahoma. Her mother, Leola Beatrice, my grandmother, lived with my great grandmother, who had eight kids. They were beyond poor, even by Oklahoma standards. She owned two dresses. Granddad had skipped out on them when Mother was little. That must have left a hole in her heart. I couldn't imagine a life without Daddy.

My dad, Willie Rathbun, was a man among men. A quiet man, he was always kind and gentle. He was also brilliant, having been admitted to Oklahoma State University at the tender age of 14. When he graduated from college at 18, he went to the war in Europe, fluent in French and German. During the war, he was an MP—a spy. After the war, he married Mother and they moved onto his daddy's Centennial farm built alongside Big Beaver Creek.

TOUGH TIMES

Daddy built the first house on the property, and then a second one after a tornado destroyed the first. Those were difficult times as people tried to rebuild a life after the war. Our farm was 11 ½ miles outside of town, so Mother had little contact with other people.

Daddy wasn't a huggy-feely type of guy, but he often walked away from his unfinished fields to go help a neighbor. When we were growing up, parents had to provide all their children's school supplies, including paper and pencils. Many couldn't afford the expense. Those folks often found bags of school supplies and food left on their porches, never knowing that it was Daddy who had left them.

The one bright spot in my life where Mother was concerned happened when I was six. May and Milton were in school, but I wasn't. So, Mother took me with her on a Greyhound bus to visit Aunt Jo and Uncle Louie in Buffalo, New York. Looking back, I wonder who was looking after four-year-old Fran while we were gone.

I have no memories of being snuggled after bath time or being read a story. Back then, there were no educational television programs. When I walked into my first-grade classroom at Comanche schools, I didn't know the alphabet or my numbers. It felt like I'd stepped into a wonderland of bright colors and books of every size and shape.

I must have learned to read at warp speed because that year, I read every one of those books. I loved school. It was easy and fun for me. I had lots of friends and social interaction. Most important, it was a wonderful reprieve from working on the farm. I didn't realize it at the time, but school was the first place in my life where I excelled and felt good about myself. It was a piece of my missing identity. To this day, learning is exciting to me.

PICNICS ON MOUNT SCOTT

On Sundays when the weather was nice, Mother fried a chicken and made potato salad. We drove to the top of Mount Scott in the Wichita Mountains and shared a family picnic. Those were wonderful times, looking out at the views and exploring the mountain,

Our family changed in a dramatic way one day when I was eight. Joyce Bandy, a lady from the Home Extension Club, arrived at our house. Mother and Joyce put their heads together stitching up something on the sewing machine. Sometime during that afternoon, Joyce led Mother to the Lord. Although her mother was a Christian, Mother had never given her heart to Jesus.

That changed everything.

From that day forward, our lives revolved around the Corum Baptist Church. Filled with sweet farm people, they welcomed us with open arms. Instead of having picnics on Sundays, we sat in church Sunday mornings, evenings and Wednesday nights. One by one, each of the rest of us gave our hearts to the Lord. To say that I loved God and the people in that church would be an understatement. Only later did I realize that at church I found another lost part of my identity.

 "It's never too early to start praying for the husband God has chosen for you," our Sunday school teacher, Mrs. Acres said. "You don't ever need to go looking for a husband. I want you to start praying every day that God will bring the right man into your life at the right time."

Music filled another missing piece of me. Fran and I were selected to be part of a group of singers made up of three sets of sisters. Not only did I love and excel at music, traveling and singing together healed something in my wounded soul.

The girls at Corum Baptist Church were part of a group known as Girls in Action. A missions discipleship organization for girls in grades one through six, we learned about missions, prayed for them and gave into their work. I still remember our pledge.

OUR PLEDGE

"Knowing that countless people grope in darkness, and giving attention to his commands, I assert my allegiance to Jesus Christ, to His church and its activities, attempting with God's help to abide in Him through prayer, to advance in wisdom by Bible study, to acknowledge my stewardship of time, money and personality, to adorn myself with good works and to accept the challenge of the Great Commission."

Each time I recited that pledge, my young heart meant every word. It helped form my foundational beliefs.

"It's never too early to start praying for the husband God has chosen for you," our Sunday school teacher, Mrs. Acres said. "You don't ever need to go *looking* for a husband. I want you to start praying every day that God will bring the right man into your life at the right time."

I prayed that prayer each day. I'm so thankful that God ignited faith in my heart to believe and obey my precious Sunday school teacher.

I was ten years old when my mother was diagnosed with terminal cancer. I didn't know much about cancer, but I understood the word terminal. When Daddy drove away, taking her to Oklahoma City where she would be treated with X-rays and radium, I didn't know if I would ever see her again.

At 14, my sister May assumed mother's role in our family. Ladies from Corum Baptist Church and the Home Extension Club also helped us. Life was harder without Mother. All four of us kids slept in the basement, and every spring the overflow from Big Beaver Creek flooded our house. The worst flooding always happened in the basement. We stacked our furniture up on concrete blocks to save them. Neighbors helped us clean up after the water receded.

DANGEROUS DOSES

When the normal levels of treatment didn't kill mother's cancer, doctors offered her another option. They could use radium at high and dangerous levels. Knowing that it was her only hope, Mother approved the treatment. Although she was gone the better part of a year, the radium eradicated the cancer, and she returned home to us. That was in 1958, the same year she took a job working at the new Haggar's Slacks Factory.

Growing up, I loved playing sports, especially softball and basketball. Softball offered base running contests. When it was my turn, I walked to home plate and kicked off my shoes. They weren't great for running, so I ran barefoot. I always won. The women's softball coach, Neal Sprouse, always laughed when I kicked off my shoes and started running. (Years later, after Ken and I married, he still laughed about it.)

I entered high school knowing that the distance from school to our farm would limit my extracurricular activities. Since I wouldn't have time to compete in sports and speech contests, I dropped sports. Kenneth Sharp, our speech teacher and coach, led our debate team all the way to state competitions. I made the national honor roll and was active in Thespians, was the Thespian Queen and secretary to the Student Council. I went to state in Triple Trio, Girl's Glee Club, Choir, One Act Play and made the All-State Cast.

If a high school student made excellent grades and turned in all their homework, they were exempted from taking final exams each semester. For me, that meant I usually didn't have to take finals. When I was 15, Comanche's exams were on a Thursday, and I didn't have to go to school. Bette Davis, one of my good friends from church who lived in nearby Walters, asked me to go to school with her that day.

I thought that sounded fun. I rode the bus with her, and each time it stopped for a student, she told me who would be getting on. We stopped in front of one house and she said, "This is where we pick up Kenny Sprouse. He's a senior. I guarantee you he's going to be singing as he gets on the bus."

A DIVINE CONNECTION

Sure enough, he did. But he stopped singing when he realized I was in his seat. We talked all the way to school and in class. It turned out we only lived seven miles apart, but somehow we'd never met. My mother had grown up in Walters and had gone to school with his mother. During music class, the teacher said, "Kenny, you can talk to her after class."

He was a handsome, blonde, blue-eyed, polite, well-mannered young man. He had an amazing ability to make people laugh. Everyone had fun when Kenny was around. I was drawn to him most because of his clever sense of humor. No matter the occasion, he always made it fun.

After school, Kenny asked what Bette and I were doing Friday evening. "We're going skating," Bette said.

Kenny and a couple of other guys met us at the skating rink. We skated and talked all evening. Before we left, Kenny asked what we'd planned for Saturday night. We were going to a youth rally to watch a Billy Graham film.

Instead of traveling in a group, he asked me out, and we double dated with another couple. Following the film, we drove over to Duncan for a soft drink. At one point, Kenny turned to look at me. "Will you marry me?"

He said it with a little laugh, but I knew he was serious. So was I.

"Yes, I will," I said.

When I prayed for my husband, I'd never imagined that it would be love at first sight. I didn't expect him to propose on our first date. He never waffled in his decision to marry me, nor did I. The more we got to know one another, the more we appreciated each other's character.

SPIRITUAL LIFE

Ken's family attended the Methodist Church in Walters. However, from the night he proposed, Ken always went to church with my family on Sunday. Since we went to different schools, we didn't see one another during the week. Although we were only seven miles apart, calling one another racked up long distance charges, something neither of our parents allowed. For the next three and a half years, we saw one another every Friday, Saturday and Sunday. During the week, we wrote letters.

During the summer of 1963, Fran and I took the Greyhound bus to Buffalo, New York to visit Aunt Jo. We had an incredible time that was over too soon. When we arrived back at the bus station in Duncan, Ken had come with Mother to pick us up. On the way home, we stopped at Bandy's Store, and someone said to Mom, "Hey! You'd better get home! Your house is on fire!"

We raced home, and when we pulled up, Neal Sprouse was already there. He was Ken's dad and the fire captain at Fort Sill. Ken and many friends helped try to put out the fire. There were no fire hydrants that far out of town, and despite our best efforts, our house was a total loss. Somehow, they'd managed to pull the freezer out of the house.

I'll never forget the sight of Daddy standing there eating frozen peaches from the freezer. As was his custom, he had total peace about the whole thing. Daddy learned early in life to be content in any situation.

Chapter Four

THE BLESSED LIFE

he sun shone like a golden orb blessing us with a benediction that August day in 1966. The campus of Central State College bustled with activity as parents helped their children move into dormitories. With great fanfare, Ken unlocked the door to our new one-bedroom apartment in married housing on campus. It was a tiny little place, but it might as well have been a palace. I was thrilled to have our first home.

That was the second happiest day of my life. The happiest day had been a few months earlier on May 28. I'd stood at the altar of Corum Baptist Church beside Ken Sprouse, agreeing to love and cherish him as long as we lived. It was a commitment I had no trouble making. I'd agreed to marry him on our first date, and my love for him had grown every day after that.

He'd graduated and enrolled at Cameron University, where he earned an associate degree in science while I finished high school. I'd graduated and earned a scholarship in music at Cameron University. By the time I arrived, Ken had graduated and moved to Edmond, Oklahoma, where he enrolled at Central State College to earn a degree in English Education. We'd decided that I should pass on my scholarship and enroll at Central State so that we'd be at the same college.

My dad, a man of few words said, "No."

That was the end of that. We honored our parents and didn't argue.

Even though Ken and I weren't married, it was his parents who helped me move into the dorm my freshman year at Cameron. They were like parents to me, helping me get settled.

I enjoyed traveling with the Cameron Singers, and I found myself the object of attention by men on campus. I wasn't interested. I'd given my heart to Ken at 15 and no one else interested me. Neither of us ever dated anyone else.

Following our marriage in May of 1966, Ken and I moved in with his parents for the summer. We each worked, saving our money for living expenses at college. We understood that once we married, financial support from our parents would stop. I figured it shouldn't take me four years to earn the 124 hours needed to earn a degree in Language Arts. I set my goal to graduate in three years.

WORKING HARD

Ken and I had parents who never said a word about hard work. They demonstrated what a good work ethic looked like, and we learned from their example. We both held jobs and worked our way through college to support ourselves. We had one car, a 1957 Chevy, but we kept it parked to save money.

We walked everywhere. Neither of us minded the extra work because we were so happy being together. I had a dream job at a Hal Owens Studio at 15th and Broadway. It was a wonderful photography studio and a great place to work.

During our second year of marriage, we were fortunate enough to get the only two-bedroom furnished apartment in college housing. The people who'd lived there before us left it in bad shape. Once again, Ken's precious mother showed up to help us clean it. Over the years, I could always count on her to sew whatever needed sewing and to mend whatever needed mending. We had a great relationship, and she was like a mother to me. Ken's parents were a beautiful part of the package God gave me with Ken.

Early in our marriage, Ken and I decided that we would never live off two salaries. We decided to budget ourselves so that we could live off just Ken's salary. We would use mine to save and make investments toward our future.

After Ken graduated, he was hired to teach at Star Spencer High School. His salary was $5,250 a year. While working full time, he also enrolled in a master's program. The war in Vietnam was raging as Ken worked toward getting his degree. At the time, if a man was married or a teacher, he received a military deferment. Since Ken was both married *and* a teacher, we were shocked when he received a draft notice.

 Early in our marriage, we decided that we would never live off two salaries. We decided to budget ourselves so that we could live off just Ken's salary. We would use mine to save and make investments toward our future.

We sat in our little apartment staring at the draft notice, knowing our lives were going to change in ways we'd never imagined. Someone knocked on the door, and we opened it to Keith Wigginton, our pastor from Highland Baptist Church. He'd never visited before, and he never came again after that day.

We welcomed him inside. "Is there anything I can pray with you about?" he asked.

"I just received a draft notice," Ken explained. "We don't want to be apart."

RED FLAG

Pastor Keith prayed with us, asking that we not be separated so early in our marriage.

Ken was 21 and in good health, so we were surprised when he failed his physical. He had high blood pressure. To his knowledge, he'd never had high blood pressure before. We were thrilled that he wouldn't be drafted, but looking back we could see that was the first red flag about his potential health problems.

When I graduated from Comanche High School in the class of 1965, ours was the largest class to ever graduate from there. As part of the Baby Boomer generation, there were always more of us competing for fewer jobs. Likewise, when I graduated from UCO, there were no teaching jobs available. I was hired to teach adult day school for pregnant girls. My salary was $5,750 a year. Those salaries convinced us that our plan to live off one salary was the only way we would ever be able to get ahead as teachers.

Later, Ken took a position teaching math, science and English for Oklahoma City Public Schools. A few months after that, he was hired as counselor at Northeast High School.

In 1970, after completing my master's degree, I was hired as an adjunct professor at the Oklahoma City campus of Oklahoma State University. Walking onto that campus felt like coming home. Somehow, God had woven education into my DNA. It was what He'd created me to do, and I reveled in it.

My boss, Phil Chandler, put me over the technical writing program. After I'd been on the job for a few months, Phil gave me a new challenge. "I want you to reimagine and transform the entire program," he explained to me one day.

As a brand-new 23-year-old professor, I didn't feel qualified to do what he was asking. I would have to decide what courses would be required for the program. Then I would have to develop the course curriculum for each of them. And then once all that was done, we would have to submit the entire program to the Board of Regents for approval. Not only did I not know how to do *any* of that, but that responsibility usually lay with the department chair.

TOO MUCH, TOO SOON

I felt I had to be upfront and honest. "I don't know how to do that," I admitted. "And isn't that typically the job of the department chair?"

Phil smiled. "Yes, but we want you to do it. We know you have the ability."

I realized that Phil saw potential in me and was willing to entrust me with challenges that would help me grow. I tackled the job and rewrote the entire program, developing courses and curriculum. Not only did the final product please my boss, but the Board of Regents gave it their stamp of approval.

I loved working with such a great boss, one who challenged me to use my gifts and talents in new ways. Over time, Phil and his wife became our friends. He joined us on many long runs. My deepest concern was that Phil was not a believer. Ken and I would chat with him about the glorious life available through Christ, but he wasn't interested. In time, we stopped talking to him about the Lord and just enjoyed the friendship. Years later, when he was in his 80s, he told me he'd given his heart to the Lord. "You just loved us," he said.

During my years at OSU, I taught at the Oklahoma City Police Academy and the Oklahoma Highway Patrol Academy. Officers received college credits for the courses they took. For the Highway Patrol, I also taught Police Records and Report Writing to every trooper. They were a fine group of young men. One year, they asked me to play the part of a trooper's wife in a movie. I'd had great speech training in school, and it was a fun experience.

One day, the director of the Oklahoma Highway Patrol Training Center asked, "Do you know why we picked you for this role?"

"No, I don't."

"Because you're the girl we would all like to take home to meet our mother."

That's about as nice a compliment as any Christian woman could get. Working with those boys was always delightful.

SAVING AND INVESTING

In 1976, Ken and I bought our first car together, which we paid off in seven months. Once it was paid off, we started making payments to ourselves, so that when we needed our next car we'd be able to pay cash.

We'd managed to save $4,700 while we were in college, which we used as a down payment to buy a little fixer-upper house. After the down payment, we only owed $13,000 on that house. That sounded good to us until we took our first look at an amortization schedule. Stunned, we realized that by the time we paid off that loan, it would cost us twice what we had spent on the house!

We decided debt wasn't our friend. Using my salary, we started paying down the principle. After spending two years fixing it up, we sold it for $25,000. From then on, we did that once a year, buying, fixing and flipping houses. We moved 16 times in the following 16 years. We put more and more in the bank after each sale.

In addition to flipping the houses we lived in, Ken got into the restaurant business. He wanted to work as a school counselor, but he needed more experience on his resume. He worked as an operations supervisor at Taco Boy, opening all their restaurants in Oklahoma. When that company folded, he spent another two years closing them.

After four years in the restaurant business, he had accumulated enough work experience to get a job as a high school counselor. While working at that job, he used the money we'd saved to buy eight Neptunes restaurants, a popular sandwich chain in the 1970s. He ran those businesses for four years before selling them at a profit. Next, he opened a Subway. Through his career as an educator, Ken opened a total of 87 restaurants!

KEN'S DAD'S DEATH

Some phone calls jangle the nerves and send a shock of dread through those who hear them. That's what this call did. It was the kind of call you never expect nor want to receive.

Ken's dad had died of a massive coronary. He was only 56 years old. While we didn't have any concerns about the state of his soul, he was far too young to die. His passing left a void in the family. We all still needed his wisdom, his laughter and his guidance.

It had been 10 years since Ken had failed his military physical. With his dad's passing, he decided it was time to get a thorough physical. He made an appointment with his father's cardiologist.

Following the exam, the cardiologist sighed. "Well, your blood pressure is high. Your cholesterol is high. Your triglycerides are high. You lost the genetic lottery, Ken. I'm sorry to say that you've inherited the same cardiovascular problems your father faced. You're a heart attack just waiting to happen."

"How do we treat it?" Ken asked.

 We traded ribs, pork and steaks for salads, fruits and whole foods. That's also when we bought our first pair of running shoes and hit the streets.

"You've got two choices. The typical approach is to put you on medications for the rest of your life. The second option is to radically change your lifestyle and try to control it with diet and exercise.

"You and I are in the same situation. I also inherited cardio-vascular problems from my father. Through diet and exercise, I've gotten my risk factors under control. It takes a lot of work and dedication, but it can be done. The choice is yours."

Being in the restaurant business, there were always mouth-watering ribs or some other delicious meal heating in our kitchen. We had access to a constant supply of wonderful foods. However, after talking through all our options, we settled on changing our lifestyle.

We traded ribs, pork and steaks for salads, fruit and whole foods. That's also when we bought our first pair of running shoes and hit the streets. Two months later, Ken went back to the cardiologist. His cholesterol was normal. His triglycerides were normal. Even his blood pressure had returned to normal. This new lifestyle became our new normal.

A SENSE OF DUTY

It wasn't too long after this change that we both took the survey which helped us realize that we'd been attending Sunday evening Bible study out of a sense of duty. Once we made the radical choice to live as though Bible was true, we read God's Word with new eyes.

Beulah Hacker, our pastor's wife at Lone Star Baptist Church, taught the Sunday school class for young marrieds. There were probably 20 people in it, which was big for a small Baptist church. On two or three different Sundays she told us, "You guys need to stop watching soap operas."

That aggravated me. During my planning period in an Oklahoma City school, I had a favorite little soap opera I enjoyed watching. The third Sunday, she said something different.

"Are you reading the Bible for as much time as you spend watching soap operas?"

That's all I needed to hear. I never watched a soap opera again. The decisions we made at that church changed our spiritual lives forever.

During that time, we started listening to Kenneth E. Hagin, Elbert Willis, Kenneth Copeland, Charles Capps, Happy Caldwell and Jerry Savelle. We didn't just listen; we looked up every scripture they taught and read it in context. They taught the uncompromised Word of God. Many people didn't receive the message because it disagreed with the traditions taught by men, teachings that were not in the Bible.

While Ken and his cardiologist inherited cardiovascular disease from their fathers, I inherited my father's amazing health and resiliency. I've never been sick and haven't had to battle sickness.

Ken, however, suffered many attacks on his health. He suffered from gallbladder disease, gout and several other major illnesses. We stood on God's Word each time, and he always received his healing. No one in health care could make that claim.

Chapter Five

THE PARTNER

K en leaned forward in his chair, meeting the eyes of the young man seated across from him in his office at a local high school. The piercings, tattoos and tough exterior hid the teen's triple-digit IQ. It masked the boy's deep, burning desire to be the first person in his family to climb out of poverty and earn a college degree.

"I know you can do this," Ken told him. "I'll make some calls and see what help you'll qualify to receive. Never give up on your dreams. With hard work and tenacity, things have a way of working out."

Ken walked him to the door and then sat down at his desk with a satisfied sigh. He loved his job, loved working with kids like this one. The other businesses—restaurants and real estate —were a means to supplement our income. Education was our first love.

At the time, we owned 14 sandwich shops in addition to our business flipping houses. Our side businesses had grown large enough that we'd brought on a partner who offered sweat equity. A very intelligent Christian businessman, he helped us with administrative details such as negotiating leases, picking up money, making deposits and handling the paperwork. It had been a wonderful relief for us to have him.

The phone rang on Ken's desk. It was our banker. "Ken, you need to do something. You're overdrawn."

"That's impossible!"

Ken listened as the banker explained the situation in detail. We weren't just overdrawn; we were in financial ruin.

The paperwork was all in order, showing each deposit and bill paid. The reality was something different. The deposits had never been made. Leases hadn't been paid. Suppliers hadn't been paid. We owed nearly $300,000 in outstanding debts, and lawsuits had been filed against us.

We were hurt and stunned that a Christian brother had brought us to the edge of destruction. Our only hope was to file for bankruptcy, but when we prayed, the Lord said, *"Get out of debt!"* He gave us no liberty to walk away from the people filing claims against us.

How were we supposed to pay off all those debts?

It seemed impossible.

STAGGERING DEBT

Our partner's wife was very ill, and we suspected that he'd become overwhelmed with his own financial crisis and took our money. We'd spent our entire marriage working extra jobs to save money and stay out of debt. Now, through no fault of our own, we found ourselves under staggering debts.

We didn't have enough capital to keep the businesses open. We shut down all but three of them. Ken went to each creditor and promised to pay off the debt, no matter how long it took. We didn't discuss the situation with anyone except our banker, our accountant and the creditors.

About that time, a friend asked if we'd ever read the book *The Laws of Prosperity* by Kenneth Copeland. We hadn't, so he loaned us his copy. Desperate for help, we studied the book and looked up every scriptural reference, reading them in context. By the time we'd read the book through the first time, we knew God had given us our answer to the financial crisis we faced.

The Lord highlighted two scriptures to us. The first was Romans 13:8, which says, "Owe no man anything, but to love one another: for he that loveth another hath fulfilled the law.

It was clear to see that the Lord didn't want us to default, nor did He want us in debt.

The second scripture He highlighted to us was Proverbs 22:7, "The rich rule over the poor, and the borrower is slave to the lender."

FINDING A WAY OUT

Ken spent months locked away, devouring every book and tape that Kenneth Copeland Ministries offered. We heard him live the first time at one of Kenneth Hagin's Camp Meetings in Tulsa. When Kenneth Copeland began holding the Southwest

Believer's Convention in Fort Worth, we attended year after year, immersing ourselves in the uncompromising Word of God. As we learned to live by faith, one thing stood out above all else:

Faith worked by love.

One evening, Ken turned to me and said, "Bea, faith works by love. We can't afford to be offended, and we can't afford to give offense."

We prayed and decided not to file legal charges against our former partner. He's spent all our money on his wife's medical bills. It was gone. While we didn't have the money to wage a legal battle anyway, even more important, we didn't think we could stay out of offense if we sued him.

We tightened our financial belt to live on my salary. We used Ken's salary to make payments on our debts. When Ken heard that our former partner's washer and dryer quit working, he bought them a new set and had them delivered.

Our former partner had signed leases for three to five years on the sandwich shops. Even though we'd closed all but three of them, and new businesses now occupied the properties, we were still obligated to pay out the terms of the leases. Only now, we were paying as much as 20 percent interest.

 One of the primary principles we learned from *The Laws of Prosperity* was Luke 6:38: "Give, and it will be given to you. They will pour into your lap a good measure—pressed down, shaken together, *and* running over. For by your standard of measure it will be measured to you in return" (NASB).

GODLY WISDOM

We owed $12,000 on one lease. Ken called and offered to settle the claim for $3,000. The man laughed. "You'll pay the entire $12,000 or I'll sue you!" Then he hung up.

Ken sat at his desk, dismayed. Someone behind him said, "Call back and offer $2,000." Ken whirled around to see who had spoken. No one was there. Although the voice sounded audible, he realized it must have been the Lord speaking.

Bewildered, Ken called the man again. "I'm calling to offer you $2,000."

"I turned down $3,000! Why would I accept $2,000?"

"I rechecked," Ken explained. "That's all I've got."

"I'm going into a meeting with a couple of the owners. I can't wait to tell them your offer. They need a good laugh today."

When he called back later, he wasn't laughing. "They accepted your offer," he said.

One of the primary principles we learned from *The Laws of Prosperity* was Luke 6:38: "Give, and it will be given to you. They will pour into your lap a good measure—pressed down, shaken together, *and* running over. For by your standard of measure it will be measured to you in return" (NASB).

GIVING OUR WAY OUT OF DEBT

"Bea," Ken said one morning, "we've got to give our way out of this." We tightened the amount we lived on until there was no breathing room at all. We spent less on groceries and other necessities. We became partners with Kenneth Copeland

Ministries and gave to them. We gave to our local church and other ministries.

At the end of the year, our accountant was flabbergasted. "You *gave* more than you *made!* This doesn't add up!"

For some reason, God always sent cars to us. During that time, we gave away seven cars. Because Ken wanted to be certain that we stayed in our love walk with our former partner, he gave the nicest one to him.

We wrote down all the scriptures from *The Laws of Prosperity* and posted them in our kitchen, bathroom and in our cars. We confessed them multiple times a day.

Still, we didn't see a way to get out from under the debt in our lifetime. We decided to stand in faith doing everything God told us to do until Jesus returned or we went the way of the grave.

We were having dinner with a couple of our friends one evening when the husband suggested that his wife and I take our children and spend the summer at their lake home. They had no idea about our financial situation; we never shared that information. I would have loved nothing more than to take the girls to the lake for the summer, but we were living off my salary. If I taught summer courses, I could earn $2,438.22. It wasn't a lot of money, but it made a big difference in our situation.

A PAID VACATION

After dinner, he slipped a check into my hand. "I'm not taking your money!" I said.

"I won't take it back," he insisted. "That check has been lying on the counter for a month. I endorsed it, but every time I picked it up to deposit it, I threw it back down. I know the money is yours."

At home that night, Ken and I looked at the check. We were stunned speechless. It was in the amount of $2,438.22. The exact amount, to the penny, that I would make teaching summer school. We knew God had arranged for me to have a paid vacation. We had a wonderful, restful summer, our husbands joining us on the weekends. I returned for the fall semester with new energy and zeal. I also had an abiding sense that our Heavenly Father was doing a perfect work in our lives.

Although we were faithful about making payments to our creditors, one man sued us for $5 million. Overwhelmed, we sought the Lord in prayer. God said, *"I've never lost a case."*

Following that word from God, we had so much peace that we didn't even show up for the court date. An attorney friend promised to go and then report back. He slipped into the back of the courtroom to watch the proceedings.

The man who was suing us got into a fight with his own attorney in court. The attorney stood up and said, "That's it! I'm leaving!"

The judge dismissed the case.

Somehow, after seven years, we had only one outstanding debt to a bank for $25,000. The day Ken made the final payment, the banker shook his head. "I know you said you'd pay this debt," he said. "But most people who say that never do."

Over a seven-year period, we paid off $267,000 of debt, not including leases and lawsuits. During that same time, we paid off the loan we'd taken against our home and all the personal debts we'd incurred.

To celebrate, I signed up to teach speed reading on a cruise. We enjoyed a free two-week Alaskan cruise. Each morning, we stood on the deck and looked at the stunning sapphire blue water, the towering mountains topped with snow, and worshipped the God of the universe. We thanked Him for his creation and for His faithfulness. We thanked Him that His mercies were new every morning.

We felt grateful not just for what He was doing *for* us. We were also grateful that He counted us worthy to include us in the story He was telling.

Chapter Six

RUNNING THE RACE

"*B*ea," Ken said with a sparkle in his eyes that told me he was up to something, "Mike and I want you to enter the Edmond 5K Turkey Trot! We think you can win us our Thanksgiving turkey. That's the trophy."

I'd set small goals for myself, like reaching a particular mailbox before stopping. I'd continued extending my distance by very small increments. One day, I burst through the front door gasping.

"I ran a mile!"

"Without stopping?" Ken asked, shocked.

"Yes!"

Ken's cousin Mike was already running. When he learned that I'd run my first mile, they entered both Kendi and me in the race.

Later, when Ken got the report from his doctor about making lifestyle changes, he joined us. We each read *The Complete Book of Running* by James Fixx, except for the last chapter. The author advised that we not read the final chapter until we were ready to run our first race.

Now that our Thanksgiving turkey was up to me, I pulled the book off the shelf and read that last chapter. He warned not to get caught up in the excitement at the start of the race and begin too fast. He advised everyone to stay at their own pace.

Thanksgiving morning, instead of baking, I found myself at the Edmond Turkey Trot. Excitement was palpable as runners crowded the starting line. Caught up in the crowd, I didn't realize that I'd started too fast until I saw my time at the end of the first mile. That's when I knew I was in trouble.

Starting too fast made the rest of the race harder, but I finished strong despite that. Kendi and I both won in our age groups! We also both won a turkey! I left that day hooked on racing.

RACING

We started racing somewhere almost every weekend. I learned to stay at my comfortable pace instead of getting swept up in the excitement and beginning too fast. After several years of collecting T-shirts, medals and trophies from all over the country, we stopped racing and just continued enjoying our local runs. Ken's mother made each of us beautiful quilts from our racing T-shirts.

I was 30 when I'd read Kenneth Cooper's book *The Aerobics Way*, which had inspired me to run and get fit. One of my friends said, "Let's run a marathon."

I'd watched the Boston Marathon on television the day before. "That's one thing I'll never do."

Never, ever say never.

All week, she kept talking about running marathons. She had a 12-week training program we could follow. You needed to be running at least 20 miles a week, but that was no problem. The problem was that I'd just given birth to Scotti and was still nursing her.

"Should I train for a marathon?" I asked Ken while we ate dinner one evening.

"Why do you keep asking me that? You can run it if you want to."

"It's going to take a lot of time."

"Don't let that be the issue. Ask God."

That was sound advice. When I prayed about it, the Lord said, *"It's fine if you train for a marathon. I'm going to teach you some things through it."*

A small group of seven of us trained for the Dallas White Rock Marathon. The schedule had us running six days a week and resting on Sunday.

THE LONG RUN

The weeks of training flew by, and we found ourselves at the starting line of the marathon the first week of December 1980. My friend Paulette and I ran together at a comfortable pace. An icy breeze sent chills all over my body, but I knew it would warm up throughout the morning. Our goal was to finish all 26.2 miles in under four hours.

The first 20 miles passed without event. We'd done a 20-mile run before, but we knew the rest of the race was beyond what we'd ever run. "This is it," Paulette said. "We've never run more than 20 miles. Do you think we can finish?"

A runner close to us heard our conversation and smiled. "Don't think of it like that," he said. You've only done 20 miles. All you've got left is a 10K! Let's do this!"

He ran on, but he'd filled our sails with wind.

We'd covered four more miles when Paulette said, "My toes are hurting. I need to stop and look at them."

"You can't stop now," I said. "If you take your shoes off, you might not be able to get them back on."

"I've got to stop."

"We've only got a little over two miles to go. If we stop it'll affect our time."

"Keep going." Paulette said, "I'll check my toes and then get back in the race."

I kept going and at mile 25, I saw Mike—walking. When I reached him, I grabbed his hand and said, "Come on, let's go!"

He'd had some kind of injury and looked at me with grim determination. "Leave. Me. Alone."

I kept running and finished in three hours and 58 minutes. It didn't feel like I'd expected. Although I was happy, I realized that the entire time the Lord had been dealing with me about being diligent to train. Whether it was running a marathon or studying God's Word, we have to be diligent to prepare.

Paulette and Mike finished just after me. Ken, who hadn't started training when we did, finished 30 minutes after me.

MEDALS, TROPHIES AND T-SHIRTS

It was a windy spring day the following year in 1981, and I was the race director for the OSU Oklahoma Marathon. As race director, I couldn't run, but Ken finished in 3:37, which was a full hour less than his previous time.

Later, Ken and I were chosen to be in a commercial. In the script, we raced to the finish line, and I was supposed to break the tape. They filmed that scene over and over to be sure they had the best shot. Kendi was seven at the time and watched the whole process. Later, I heard her tell someone, "My mom won every time, but I know my dad could have."

Ken and I, like many couples, had our own little meaningful habits and traditions. Anytime we flew on an airplane, one of us ordered cranberry juice and the other ordered ginger ale. Then we mixed them and made our little cocktail, toasting one another. As soon as our plane reached altitude on our flight to San Francisco, we made our cranberry-ginger ale cocktail to celebrate the trip.

 "I started running years ago after reading your book," I told Kenneth Cooper.

It was a stunning morning in San Francisco that day in 1982. Ken, Mike and I were there to run the Bay to Breakers race. The vivid blue sky mirrored the water in the bay. Soft white clouds meandered like dandelions on the wind. I'd never seen such excitement as 65,000 people gathered to run. The majority of them were in costumes, making it the most fun race on the planet.

The next year, 1983, Ken and I mixed our cranberry-ginger ale on the long flight to Hawaii. We toasted one another, excited to land on the big island. We'd registered to run the Honolulu Marathon.

OH, WHAT A BEAUTIFUL MORNING

At six o'clock in the morning, fireworks filled the sky, the starting gun went off and the race began. My boss and his wife joined Ken and me for the marathon. It was a beautiful morning as we ran past palm trees. The course took us alongside the ocean, the crisp smell of the sea on a gentle breeze. It was an exhilarating adventure, unlike anything we'd done before. One of those experiences we'd never forget.

As I ran through the finish line, at a good steady pace, I knew that it was one marathon I wouldn't repeat. Although I enjoyed running at sea level and the stunning views, I wasn't used to the heat. It was stifling.

Then, the first time we ran the Oklahoma City Marathon, I only ran half, as we were running Dallas' White Rock Marathon in two weeks. The following year, I ran the entire 26.2 miles and won in my age group. In 2007, my sister Fran and her friend Teresa were going to run the Austin Marathon. I decided to join them. It was a beautiful but hilly course. The three of us stayed together the whole time until about mile 25, where you circle the Texas Capital and head for the finish line.

When I saw that, I said, "Girls, I've got to take off!" They followed, which allowed them to meet their time goal. We all enjoyed running the Austin Marathon.

Years later, when Kendi and Scotti registered to become certified aerobics instructors at the Cooper Institute in Dallas, they
urged me to join them. I went, because participating in something at the Cooper Institute was a dream come true. I
received my certification as an aerobics instructor as well.
During one class, taught by Kenneth Cooper himself, we sat
on the front row.

"I started running years ago after reading your book," I told
him after class.

"And now you have your daughters here with you," he replied.
What a wonderful experience and an inspirational man.

Over the years, we added many types of exercise to our regi-
men. We taught aerobics, lifted weights, did circuit training,
participated in boot camps, walked, rode bicycles and took
Kenpo karate classes. We also added Jazzercise and Body and
Soul classes.

In addition to all the health benefits, I always enjoyed the
camaraderie with our workout buddies.

Chapter Seven

PASSING THE TORCH

I felt a chill ripple up my spine as I stood on the banks of Waurika Lake. Gazing across the blue water, peaking with little whitecaps as the wind whipped it into a frenzy. It felt strange knowing that the creation of this lake meant the end of an era in our family.

Hidden beneath the surface of the water lay our Centennial Farm. Our home. Our property. The fields where we once picked cotton. The place where we loved and laughed. The pecan trees we harvested and climbed. A lifetime of memories, buried in a watery grave.

There had been a lot of talk during my childhood that the government might dam up Big Beaver Creek and Little Beaver Creek, both tributaries of the Red River, to form a lake. Most folks didn't think it would ever happen, my father among them.

We four kids were all grown with families of our own when the U.S. Army Corps of Engineers finally constructed their dam to create a lake. Waurika Lake would provide water for Duncan, Comanche, Temple and Waurika, Oklahoma.

Over the course of a few weeks in 1980, our beloved property would go from being a productive farm to a lake bottom. No one who owned property in the area had a vote. They didn't have the choice to opt out. Daddy was losing his farm. Period. End of story.

Of course, they were paid, but the price wasn't negotiable. If Daddy had been a different kind of man, he might have been devastated. He might never have gotten over it. He might have been angry, bitter and depressed.

That wasn't who he was.

Daddy didn't want to move, but he never got upset.

He pondered the situation and saw no way of getting around it. He kept his peaceful, happy countenance. If the truth be known, Mother kind of wanted off the farm. It was a beautiful place to live, but a tremendous amount of work. It was getting hard for them to keep up with it.

Our house had burned down, been hit by a tornado, and it still flooded every year. Now this. Each of us had gone home to collect anything we wanted. Mother and Daddy had packed their belongings and moved into a three-bedroom brick house in Meridian.

THE FAMILY LINE

In 1978, Neal, Ken's dad, died of a sudden heart attack. We'd invited Ken's mother Leona, whom we all called MeMe, to move in with us. She wouldn't leave as long as Neal's father, Garland was still alive.

Two years later, Garland was in the hospital and not expected to live. We were concerned because he'd never made a profession of faith. We drove to Lawton praying that God would clear his hospital room so that we'd have time alone with him.

When we arrived, family members had crowded into the room. But, one by one, they left until it was just Garland and us. "We've come to talk to you about Jesus," Ken said, getting right to the point.

"Well, I don't know about that," Garland said.

"What is it that bothers you?" Ken asked.

"You don't know how bad I've been."

"You don't know how powerful the Blood of Jesus is to remove all trace of sin."

We continued to minister to him and led him to the Lord.

Back home, we wondered if perhaps he'd just parroted the words without any belief in his heart. At the memorial service, Pastor Weldon Rightner said, "You know, I went by to visit Garland all the time. I tried to get him to pray the prayer of salvation, but he never would.

"Last week when I arrived, Garland told me, 'Preacher, I prayed that prayer with my grandkids!'" Garland had been happy to share the news.

AROUND THE WORLD OR ACROSS STATE LINES

Many years later, we were on warp speed trying to get everything ready to fly to India on Monday morning. The Saturday before we left, Ken's Aunt Mary called from a hospital in Fort

Worth and asked us to come see her. Mary was Ken's dad's sister and Garland's daughter.

"I don't see a way for us to go," Ken admitted. We weren't concerned about her spiritual condition, because she'd lived with us and gone to church with us.

"I know what you mean about our schedule," I told Ken. "But if we can fly to the other side of the world to minister to strangers, we can make the time to drive to Fort Worth for Aunt Mary."

Her hospital room was packed when we arrived, but one by one, people left and we found ourselves alone with her. She got right to the point. "You know that prayer you prayed with Daddy? Would you pray it with me?"

We had no idea she had never prayed the prayer of salvation.

Meanwhile, after surviving cancer in 1958, my mother had lived a long life. Over the next 40 years, she suffered a series of health issues which I suspected might have been the result of the high dose of radium she'd taken to rid her body of cancer.

For years she'd said, "If I could just live until I'm 70."

Back then, 70 was considered old. When I learned that the Bible said that we can have whatever we say, I cringed when she said she wanted to live to 70. I wanted her to live longer than that.

FACING CANCER AGAIN

In 1994, she was diagnosed with pancreatic cancer and given two weeks to two months to live. She survived almost two more years.

God knew I was going to try and get her healed by His Word, and He warned me off. *"Don't challenge your mother."*

His warning made me realize that she wouldn't accept her healing. If I challenged her, it would make the last of her life harder.

Mother didn't want to die in the hospital or in a nursing home. She wanted to die at home. She had us put a hospital bed in the living room. Her mind was sharp, and she ruled the world from that bed. None of us lived close, but we set a schedule so that we took turns staying with her. When none of us could be there, we hired people to help.

One cold morning I arrived, and Mother had planned our day. "I want you to take me to the funeral home to make arrangements."

We arrived at the funeral home, and I discovered she knew just what she wanted, down to the last song and order of service. Her heart's desire was for Fran, me and the two other sets of sisters who sang together as children to sing at her funeral.

We all lived in different parts of the country. We couldn't be sure of whether we could all make it to the funeral. So, we set a date and recorded the songs Mother wanted us to sing. The recording would be played at her service.

While we were at the funeral home, Mother planned Daddy's funeral too. He was quite a bit older than her and couldn't live alone if she weren't there.

PRIDE IN HER VOICE

A few months later, it was a stunning day in Spring, and I'd opened the patio door so Mother could enjoy the fresh breeze.

Back then in rural Oklahoma, doctors still made house calls. When her doctor arrived, I stepped out onto the patio and shut the screen door so they could have privacy.

"That's my daughter," Mother said with pride. "She's the college professor."

I froze when I heard those words. She sounded proud, happy with my success. I realized she had already told him about me.

She'd never said anything like that to me. In my whole life, she'd never praised me. She'd never encouraged me or acted like anything I'd done mattered.

I stood in the soft morning sun and let those words seep into the broken places of my heart. The heart that had yearned for her love for so long. I stood unmoving, knowing that what I heard was a gift from God. He wanted me to hear those words before she left this earth.

Mother wasn't afraid of death. She had great peace through the whole process. She'd been a good friend to many people over the years, and they were faithful to visit her now. She held court from her bed in the living room.

We'd all said our goodbyes and promised to take care of Daddy. An ice storm hit the week of Thanksgiving 1996. Icicles hung from the roof. Tree limbs cracked from the weight of the ice. Ice covered the streets. The world felt shrouded, entombed in an igloo of ice.

My brother Milton, my sister Fran and Daddy were with her when Mother slipped the bonds of earth and went to worship at the throne of God. She had turned 70 on September 28 that year. She died the week of Thanksgiving.

FINDING A PLACE FOR DADDY

Once Mother was gone, we all knew Daddy couldn't stay alone. Each of us wanted him to come live with us. A man of few words, he said, "No."

My sister lived in Chickasha, and she suggested that he move into a nursing home close to her. We drove him to visit. He said, "No."

We drove him home, asking God for a solution. We were between Duncan and Comanche when Daddy said, "I'd like to live there."

He pointed to a nursing home that bordered his and Mother's property. For years, Daddy had walked over to visit. I turned in and discovered that they had a room available. Daddy moved in that same day.

A week later, I went to visit him. "Are you happy here?"

A sweet smile creased his face. "I've learned it's best to just be content wherever you are."

We arrived to visit once and found Daddy calming a violent patient. "Has your father always been this way?" the nursing home director asked.

"Always," I said. He lived his life in a calm peace. I'd never once seen him upset or angry.

I prayed that when his time came, Daddy would slip away in his sleep. As peaceful in death as he'd always been in life. I didn't know until later that all of my siblings had been praying the same prayer.

One morning the nursing home director phoned me. "I'm sorry to tell you, but your dad died last night in his sleep."

All I could say was, "Praise the Lord."

At my parents 50th anniversary celebration at Corum Baptist Church, Merle Lambert, one of Daddy's lifelong friends said, "I've never known Willie Rathbun to say a negative thing about anybody."

I wished that could be said about me.

GOING HOME AGAIN

Oklahoma is not immune to drought, and the one that hit the summer of 2011 was worse than most. It was so dry that many small towns were on the verge of dying if it didn't rain soon.

"Bea," my brother, Milton, sounded excited when he called, "if you want to see the old homestead, come home. The drought is so bad the lake is dry. We can walk our property."

It felt like living a dream when we stepped on that lakebed, dry as chalk. None of us imagined we'd ever get to go home again. At least, not to that homestead. We found the foundation of the house. We walked across what had once been cotton fields. We stood at the site of our barn and remembered the fun when our cow gave birth to twins.

Memories. Everywhere we turned. Each of us found a treasure to take home. Mother and Daddy seemed close enough to touch. It was an experience none of us ever thought we'd get to have. To us, it was a gift from God. One last chance to go home.

It started to rain soon after our visit. The headlines on the front page of the *Comanche Times* read, **A *Miracle of Biblical Proportions.*** Once it started raining, Waurika Lake filled in only one week.

That day on the dry lakebed, I remember standing where our front porch once stood. I thought about all those dear departed ones who'd passed the torch to us. My earliest memories were of holidays at my great grandmother's home. The table always laden with a bounty of food and her home overflowing with an abundance of love.

For the first 31 years of my life, we enjoyed five generations on my mother's side of the family. My great grandmother didn't die until I was 31. As my grandparents aged, the family shifted to my parents' house for the holidays. Now the torch had been passed to me and my siblings.

They passed the torch of the love of God and the Church. They passed the torch of what it means to be family. They passed the torch of what it meant to love and be loved. Now it was our turn to keep that flame alive.

Chapter Eight

NO SMELL OF SMOKE

T loved my job at OSU and was only one year away from being fully vested. That's why Ken and I were so surprised at the next direction we received from God.

"Quit your jobs and start a school."

Quit? One year from becoming vested? Quit both of our jobs, our chief means of income?

Living a life of faith was never boring. What God asked us to do seemed illogical to the natural mind. But we'd had years to develop ears to hear that still, small voice. Even so, I had reservations.

Ken shifted in an instant and was ready to obey God. I drug my feet for three days. Our daughters attended the best private school in Oklahoma City. The quality of their education was next to none. Yet I knew if we started a school, we'd have to pull them out of Casady and enroll them in ours. I felt they were in the right place for a great education. How could I pull them out?

I sought the Lord about it. On the third day, I went for a long run by myself. I wasn't so much praying as whining to God. I heard a voice behind me so loud that I turned around to see who had spoken. No one was there, except the Lord. He spoke in the loudest voice I'd ever heard Him use.

"Do you know that I love your girls more than you do? I would never ask you to do anything that wasn't good for them."

That was all I needed to hear. I was on board.

Having bachelor's and master's degrees, we had a high priority on academic excellence. We figured we'd been called to start a school because of all our years in education.

"That's not why I picked you," the Lord said. *"You know the world's way. I'm going to show you My way."*

The first thing He directed us to do was *not* to advertise for students.

We never advertised for 30 years. I'm always amazed at what God can do in three days. He brought Jonah out of the belly of the whale. He brought Jesus out of hell. And he changed my attitude.

A DIFFERENT NAME

We'd helped our pastors, Rickey and Karla Musgrove, start God's Light Shining Church, and we'd been the children's pastors for 10 years. We assumed that the school God instructed us to build would be a part of the church. We planned on calling it God's Light Shining Christian School.

As Ken walked up the steps to the state office to register the name, the Lord spoke.

"The name of the school will be Edmond Christian Academy."

"Lord," Ken replied, "that name won't be available."

But it was. Ken registered the school under that name.

The school would be in Edmond, but we lived in a neighborhood called Ski Island in Oklahoma City. We started driving around Edmond looking at land to build a home. One day we found two lots near Coltrane that we liked. Ken called the banker who owned them.

"Nobody wants to take a chance on those lots because they need a retaining wall and dirt work," the banker explained.

Retaining walls and dirt work didn't bother us. We got a great deal on those lots. Once we got the dirt work done, people often stopped by to admire them. "Those are the most beautiful lots in the neighborhood," they said.

When we put our house in Ski Island up for sale, it sold in a single weekend. While that was great, it also meant that we didn't have anywhere to live during the nine months it would take to build our new house. We bought a lot on the corner of Western Avenue and Coffee Creek through a sheriff's sale for $900. We bought a used mobile home for $3,000. It needed a lot of work to make it livable. Ken joked about the size. "You can vacuum the whole house without unplugging the vacuum cleaner!"

TEACH ME YOUR WAYS

During the nine months that we lived there, we drove up and down Western Avenue every day. Each day we passed 12 acres for sale. One day Ken said, "We need to buy that property."

"Honey, what would we do with it?" I asked. As far as I was concerned, we had more than enough on our plate.

Still, every day as we drove past it, he said, "We need to buy that property." I stopped arguing. On the outside, I pretended to agree. But inside, I still opposed the idea. In time, Ken stopped talking about it.

Our lives were so busy that we always guarded our sleep. But while living in that mobile home, God woke Ken every night for two weeks to give him new revelation. The first night it happened, the Lord told him, "*Let me teach you about Matthew 24.*"

"Lord, I've already taught on Matthew 24."

That night, the Lord gave him a deeper revelation of that chapter than Ken had ever known or heard. The next morning, instead of being exhausted, he felt rested.

That continued happening night after night as God downloaded more revelation about His Word. One evening, Ken didn't even bother going to bed. He stayed up all night learning from the Holy Spirit. There was so much warfare that he woke me to help pray. After praying and warring with him for a while, I went back to bed.

Afterwards, the Lord said, *"You are going to start a work named Edmond Christian Center. It won't be just a church. It will also be a place for Christian activities."*

Because of the name, Edmond Christian Center, we knew we were to start the church and school in Edmond. We looked all over town for a place to lease but found nothing. We decided to build and started looking at land.

"Ken," I finally agreed, "we need to buy that property on Western!"

MAKING A DEAL

Ken called and discovered someone else had already made an offer on it. He called back and asked, "Have the buyers put money down on the land?"

"No, actually, they haven't," the owner said.

They were asking $33,000 for the 12 acres. We prayed and believed that the property was ours. Ken called the owner and told him we were building a church and believed the property was ours.

The other buyers were building a church and believed the property was theirs.

The owner called his father, who was a pastor. "I've got two churches who both want to buy the property," he said. "What should I do?"

"Does either of them have the money?"

"One of them does."

"Sell it to the man with the money."

TRIAL BY FIRE

The land was bare, just a thicket.

We needed a lot of dirt work on all those acres. A friend gave us some sound advice. "You need to sell the dirt. You'll get paid and get your dirt work done for free."

We posted a sign that we had dirt for sale.

We made more money on the sale of the dirt than we paid for the property.

Another business approached us about putting a cell tower on our property. They paid us for selling air!

We didn't start the building until July, but somehow, we opened the doors of Edmond Christian Academy on time for the fall semester. Several doors inside the building hadn't been hung. The ceiling tiles weren't in. The carpet hadn't been laid. But we celebrated God's faithfulness with each new student.

The whole family was excited as we climbed into our new compact Chevy for the second day of school. The first day had been hectic, but I knew things would start settling down into a routine today.

We were northbound on May Avenue approaching the intersection at 164th with farmland in every direction. As we headed north, from the west we saw a car barreling toward us. It didn't show any signs of slowing down or stopping. It looked like it was going to run the stop sign.

"Don't do it! Don't do it!" Ken shouted, aghast that the driver might run the stop sign.

I turned to check on the girls and that loosened my seatbelt. The jolt of the crash threw me forward. I felt the impact of my head hitting the windshield, the screaming sound of metal being crushed and glass breaking. Our car was knocked down a deep ravine, landing at the bottom with a crashing boom.

The second impact seemed to implode our car as the other vehicle went over the side of the ravine, plunging down on top of us.

The sudden silence seemed eerie.

Ken climbed out of the wreckage unharmed.

Scotti climbed out unharmed.

Then Kendi climbed out unharmed.

Blood poured from wounds on my face and head as I tried to stop the flow to protect our new car. Ken looked inside and said, "Don't bother, Honey. The car's totaled. You're not going to like the way your face looks."

I looked at the windshield and realized that my head had broken it. Lacerations crossed my forehead in a lateral position, and another went upwards into my scalp. Both wounds so deep it exposed the bone.

Ken helped me out of the car as a highway patrolman circled the wreckage. He'd been going south on May Avenue and had witnessed the wreck. Ken asked him to call Rickey Musgrove to come help us. We knew everyone at the school must be frantic, because we were always the first to arrive. They all knew that only something like this would make us late.

The driver who ran the stop sign was a 16-year-old girl.

"Mom," Kendi said, "we need to pray for that girl. She's all alone."

We walked over and prayed for her. When Rickey arrived, he took Ken to the school. I was strapped onto a wooden board and loaded into the back of an ambulance. The girls, 14 and 6, rode up front.

UNBROKEN BONES

At the hospital, they sat in the waiting room while I was treated. An X-ray showed that my nose was broken. On the advice of one of the nurses, we asked for a plastic surgeon to suture my face.

Having gotten everyone started at school, Ken and Rickey arrived at the hospital. "Can I touch your nose?" Rickey asked.

By now, everything throbbed with pain. "No," I told him.

 No one will ever know there were stitches. There won't be a single scar.

— MAXINE POTTER

He put his hand close to my nose and prayed for healing.

When the plastic surgeon arrived, they did more tests and X-rays. The medical staff seemed confused. "This shows that your nose isn't broken."

It *had* been broken on the first X-ray.

Something was wrong with the numbing medicine. It didn't numb anything but caused my face to swell, making the situation harder for the surgeon and more painful for me. When they finished, my head was wrapped like a mummy.

"I'm ready to go to school," I told Ken.

"You're not going to school."

Ken took me home to rest, then he and the girls went back to school.

When they got home that evening, Kendi crawled up on my bed and put her head on my chest. With a deep sigh she said, "I'm tired of being strong."

That night, after the girls were in bed, Ken and I looked at each other with knowing eyes. "The devil tried to take us out," Ken said.

"Yes, he did, but he didn't succeed."

Our friend, Maxine Potter, prophesied, "No one will ever know there were stitches. There won't be a single scar."

There wasn't. Even today, looking into a well-lit mirror, I can't find a scar. The devil gave it his best shot, but like the Hebrew boys Shadrach, Meshach and Abednego who were thrown in a fiery furnace, God brought us out of our fiery trial without so much as the smell of smoke.

Chapter Nine

BRANNON AND KENDI

J peeked into Kendi's bedroom just as Ken finished praying with her and tucking her into bed. The lamp on her bedside table cast a warm glow over her sleepy smile. She knew what was coming. Sitting on the side of her bed, Ken sang "18 Yellow Roses" to her.

He reached the end and sang, "I guess there's nothin' left for me to do but ask to meet the boy that's done this thing. And find out if he's got plans to buy you a ring. 'Cause eighteen yellow roses will wilt and die one day, but a father's love will never fade away."

He sang a lot of songs to the girls over the years, but that was the most consistent and the most meaningful. He sang it to both of them at bedtime. He sang it to them in the car on the way to school. He sang it at the table during meals. He sang it on holidays.

The girls knew their daddy loved them. They knew we both loved them. We wanted the best for them, and that included a godly mate. I believed then, and still do, that some of the best advice that I'd ever been given was to pray for God to bring my husband to me.

That's why Ken and I started praying for their spouses while they were still in the womb. As soon as they were old enough to pray for themselves, we taught them to pray for their husbands.

As youth pastors, we'd taught the youth the same thing we taught our girls. You don't have to date and kiss a lot of frogs to find your mate. You don't need to chase after anyone. You can pray and trust God to bring your spouse at the right time.

Although Kendi wasn't homeschooled, many of her friends were. When she was 16, one of them invited her to attend the Homeschool Christmas Banquet.

Brannon Golden wasn't a homeschool student either, but one of his friends from church invited him to the same Christmas banquet. He was 19, had graduated from high school, tested out of freshman comp and scored high on his ACT exam.

They fell for one another in an instant, a lot like Ken and I did. A member of Hopewell Church, Brannon had also been taught to pray and believe God for his mate.

Brannon started attending our church and spending a lot of time at our house. He and Kendi spent time with their youth group, getting together for pizza.

TRUSTING BRANNON

Brannon had been around a lot, and Ken had gotten to know him. One evening I asked Ken where we were supposed to pick up Kendi after pizza. "Brannon is bringing her home."

"Are you okay with that?"

"Yes," Ken said. "He's going to love and take care of her. We can't ask for more."

We didn't know Brannon's family, but we wanted to get to know them. His parents, Connie and Mo Golden, invited us to dinner. We had a wonderful time with them. On the way home, I said, "Isn't that neat? They're just nice, normal people like us."

"They're nice," Kendi agreed, "but we aren't normal, and neither are they."

There may have been a hint of truth to that.

At 16, Kendi graduated from high school early and with honors. She enrolled at Oklahoma City University with elementary education as her major. Over the next two years, Scotti who was 8, glued herself to Kendi and Brannon. They didn't date, but Scotti didn't let them have any privacy.

"When Scotti finds her guy," Brannon said, "we're going to hire a 10-year-old kid to go everywhere with them."

Although they knew they would marry, Brannon didn't want to get engaged until he could afford a ring.

 One evening over dinner, Brannon mentioned in passing, "I'd love to get a master's degree in technical writing from Rensselaer, but I know I can't."

"Why not?" Kendi asked. "Of course, you can."

"What would you like for Christmas?" he asked Kendi one year.

"I want to make our engagement official," Kendi replied. "I don't need a ring."

Brannon wrote a beautiful letter to the church, declaring his love for Kendi and his intention to marry her. The day the letter was read to the church, he had 18 yellow roses front and center on the stage. She was thrilled.

A NEW PATH

They married while Kendi was still in college. She graduated with honors in only three years at age 19. In addition to her bachelor's degree in elementary education, she later became Spanish certified for elementary education.

Although we were educators with college degrees, it didn't bother us at all that Brannon didn't have one. We loved his heart for God and our daughter. He'd attended OSU for a while after graduating from high school, but he didn't like it and dropped out.

The more I got to know him, the more convinced I was that he'd been given bad advice when he enrolled. Because he was brilliant, they'd put him on a path for engineers. He wasn't made for that. He was a great writer. "Brannon," I said, "you need to get a technical writing degree from OSU/OKC."

He decided to try it and loved it, excelling at the program. After earning his associates degree in just two semesters, he enrolled at UCO and earned his bachelor's degree in English. One evening over dinner, Brannon mentioned in passing, "I'd love to get a master's degree in technical writing from Rensselaer, but I know I can't."

"Why not?" Kendi asked. "Of course you can."

Rensselaer was a college in Albany, New York, considered the best program for technical writing in the country. It had never occurred to Brannon that Kendi would do anything to help him fulfill his dreams.

Brannon had a brochure from Rensselaer with an information request card on it. Kendi sent it in, then filled out all the paperwork and submitted it. After taking the GRI, Brannon was accepted into their graduate program. Next, she began searching for a teaching job. There were many small states within driving distance of Albany, but she wasn't sure if her teaching certificate would transfer. She called the State Board of Education for each state and got a recording every time.

STEPPING OUT ON FAITH

Until she called Vermont. A person answered the phone, and during the conversation she explained that the state of Vermont and the state of Oklahoma had a reciprocity agreement. That meant that they would honor one another's teaching certifications. She searched for a job and found an opening for a fifth-grade teacher in North Bennington, Vermont. It was about 30 minutes from Albany.

She applied for the job. The principal called the following Monday and explained that if she wanted to interview for the position, she should be at the school on Friday. They had scheduled 10 in-person interviews that day.

Kendi was out of school for the summer while Brannon worked. They both wanted to go, but they didn't have enough money. Kendi had the interview, so it made sense for her to go alone.

The flight to New York City cost $1,200, but I had frequent flier miles that allowed her to fly free roundtrip. She rented a car and then got a map and planned her route from New York City to North Bennington, Vermont. She wrote the route out, and to be sure she didn't make a mistake, she memorized it.

Meanwhile, she'd been searching the computer for a place to live and came up with nothing. It was tough. They only needed a rental for nine months, the term of the school year. They didn't want to bring their furniture, so they needed something furnished. They did want to bring their cat, so pets had to be approved. There was nothing close to what they needed.

Then she found it. A stunning 100-year-old home. The owners, an attorney and a professor, were traveling to India for nine months where the wife was considering a research study. They wanted to rent their house, furnished, to someone who would take care of their dog and three cats.

Kendi flew to New York City, then drove to North Bennington, where she looked at the house. She loved it. She went for her interview and was told, "We'll let you know."

"Mom," she told me after her interview, "I'm going to rent that house."

"Don't you need a job first?"

"That would be plan B."

What could I say? We'd always taught the girls that faith had no plan B.

She rented the house and flew home.

HOME IN VERMONT

When the principal called, it was with good news. She'd gotten the job.

Toward the end of July, Brannon was offered a scholarship to Rensselaer. It had been granted to someone who had turned it down. They gave it to Brannon even though he hadn't applied for one.

They left from our driveway, so excited about their adventure that they couldn't stop grinning. Ken and I had total peace, assured that they were following the leading of the Lord. We saw His fingerprints on the entire process.

They took both cars, loaded with their personal belongings and their cat. The first week in North Bennington, Kendi was at the neighborhood grocery store when someone said, "You must be the new fifth grade teacher."

"Yes, I am. How did you know?"

"You're a stranger," as though that said it all. It was a very small, close-knit community and both Brannon and Kendi loved it. Kendi enjoyed the school and fell in love with her students. Brannon enjoyed his classes, which met from Monday through Friday. They spent each weekend exploring New England.

Brannon's parents, Connie and Mo, visited in October.

Over Thanksgiving, we took Scotti, her friend Stacy, Ken's mom, MeMe, and my great Aunt Gracie and drove to Niagara Falls. It was fabulous to watch the powerful display of God's creation. I'd seen pictures, but they didn't do it justice. I stood close enough to feel the spray as 3,000 tons of water poured over the falls every second.

I felt tiny, insignificant in the face of the power before me. The force of the water, the roar of the falls and the massive sky above made me ever so aware of God's supreme power. His majesty. To wonder that the God who created this, died for me.

It took my breath away.

After tearing ourselves away, we went to Brannon and Kendi's beautiful gingerbread house. We all helped cook and had a delightful holiday.

As the year progressed, Kendi fell more in love with her students and the school. She hadn't told them that she would only be there for one school year. Now she wondered how she would break the news.

HOME AGAIN

As it turned out, she didn't have to. The enrollment was down for the upcoming school year. They had to let one teacher go, and Kendi was the newest. She was the last teacher whose contract had been signed. The school couldn't renew her contract.

Kendi was still teaching when Scotti graduated from high school early at age 16. She and Brannon couldn't come home for the graduation, but we all went to Albany for Brannon's graduation from Rensselaer. His degree opened the way for many jobs nationwide. We didn't know where they would go from there, but Brannon broke the suspense.

"We love it here," he said, "but we're ready to go home."

Back in Oklahoma, Brannon worked as a technical writer for a company and Kendi taught fourth grade at Washington Irving Elementary. The Lord had led them to join Life Church, back when it only had two campuses. Founded by Pastor Craig Groeschel, it grew to have 44 locations in eight states. Scotti also attended there.

Ken used to tease the staff at Life Church. "I sent my girls to your church as missionaries!"

"That's the truth, Ken. Those girls of yours know God's Word!"

In 2002, when Rick Warren's book *The Purpose Driven Life* came out, we all read it at the same time. While reading the book, Kendi had a revelation from God.

"You're supposed to be writing curriculum."

She'd never known that.

WALKING IT OUT

She did know that there was an opening at Life Church for someone to write curriculum for children. "Mom," she said, "I think I'm supposed to have that job."

She applied, but the position had already been filled. As the new school year approached, we helped her move everything into her classroom. A day or two before school started, she got a call from Life Church.

"The person we hired to write curriculum quit."

She interviewed for the position and got the job. We helped her pack up her classroom.

I enjoyed watching her turn to Ken. "Help me figure out the best way to teach this complicated truth to children." The two of them put their heads together and worked it out.

Meanwhile, Brannon was on his way to work one morning when the Lord interrupted his drive. *"I want you to quit your job."*

Brannon was so surprised that he pulled over, stopped and called Kendi.

Brannon started his own business and stayed busy working countless hours. One of his clients was Life Church. Bobby Gruenewald had created a Bible app called YouVersion, which made the Bible available on Android, iOS, Windows phones and many other operating systems. Life Church offered it for free. It is the number one Bible app in the world, with over half a billion downloads worldwide. Through his business, Brannon contracted writing for YouVersion.

STEPPING INTO HIS CALL

When a job opening became available writing for YouVersion in 2014, Kendi quizzed Brannon. "Aren't you going to apply for that job?"

Brannon shrugged. "If they wanted me, they would have mentioned it."

"How would they know you were interested?"

That was a good point. Brannon inquired about the opening. "We didn't know if you would be interested since you own your own business."

Brannon accepted the job with joy because it touched so many lives.

Kendi has worked for Life Church since 2003. For many years, she was the Central Team Leader for Content, but now is Head of Content for YouVersion. She also visits the 44 campuses nationwide to encourage and uplift them.

She has never forgotten her students in Vermont. They traveled back to North Bennington to celebrate with them when Kendi's class graduated from eight grade. They went back again to celebrate their graduation from high school.

Chapter Ten

DAMIAN AND SCOTTI

The celebration for Scotti's 21st birthday fell a little flat. "I'd rather not marry than marry the wrong man," she told me. I couldn't help but wonder if she'd given up her dream of finding the kind of love that Ken and I had. She'd had a front row seat when God brought Brannon and Kendi together.

It hadn't happened for her.

Scotti had prayed the same prayers that I'd prayed. She'd prayed the same prayers that Kendi prayed. I'd met Ken when I was only 15. Kendi had met Brannon when she was 16. Scotti just assumed that it would happen that way for her too.

Now, at 21, she seemed to put those dreams on a shelf. She made it clear that she didn't want any more well-meaning friends introducing her to guys. Like Kendi, she'd graduated early at 16 and earned a full scholarship to college.

On their first day at UCO, some fraternity boys invited Scotti and her friend Stacy to a party.

"We don't date," they said.

She earned her bachelor's degree in early childhood education and graduated at 19 without ever meeting her mate.

She earned her master's degree as a reading specialist. She still hadn't met her mate.

With a steady income from teaching, she'd moved out of our house and bought one of her own. God still hadn't brought her a godly mate. If it was any consolation, she wasn't alone. While most of the young people she knew who'd prayed instead of dating had met and married by this time, Sarah, Stacy and Scotti were the exceptions.

ROMANCE IN PARIS

We'd planned to take a group of students to Europe on a two-week educational tour. A month before we left, Sean told Ken that he wanted to propose to Sarah while they were there.

"Well, if you want to do that, the grandest place would be at the top of the Eiffel Tower," Ken explained. "But you can't propose on the trip if you haven't already asked her parents. That's the first thing you need to do."

As weeks passed, Ken continued asking Sean if he'd talked to Sarah's parents yet.

He hadn't.

The night before we left, he gathered up enough nerve to talk to them.

Everyone on the trip knew his plans except Sarah.

The day we were scheduled to visit the Eiffel Tower, the engagement ring was burning a hole in Sean's pocket. When we finally arrived, *the tower was closed!*

Sean deflated like a flat tire. We all felt so sorry for him.

"I guess I'll propose at the Louvre," he said.

"No," I insisted. "Just wait."

We rescheduled some things and visited the Eiffel Tower another day.

It was open!

Reaching the top of the Eiffel Tower, a panoramic view of Paris spread before is in every direction. We saw the River Seine bisecting the most romantic city on earth. In the distance was Notre Dame and the Arc de Triomphe, but none of us could focus on the view.

All our attention was on Sean as he dropped to one knee, held up the ring and proposed. I'll never forget the look on Sarah's face. What an amazing experience.

Back home, Arturo proposed to Stacy.

FINDING SCOTTI'S MATE

Two weeks after Scotti's 21st birthday, she attended a Bible study. Afterwards, she called and said, "I've met the man I'm going to marry. He's divorced and has a four-year-old daughter."

They'd both known instantly that they would marry.

Just like Ken and me. Just like Brannon and Kendi.

However, Damian's divorce was difficult for us. We'd never entertained the idea of divorce and couldn't imagine it for our daughter. However, the Lord stood up for Damian. He told us, "If my blood isn't enough to cover Damian's past, it's not enough for yours either."

That settled it for both of us.

THE BLOOD IS ENOUGH

When Damian introduced himself at the Bible study that night, he'd said, "I'm Damian Wilson. I'm divorced, and my four-year-old daughter is the love of my life."

A week later, Scotti hosted a dinner party so we could meet Damian. Of course, we loved him. He was everything we'd ever hoped for in a son-in-law. He loved the Lord and loved our daughter. He played the guitar and worshipped God from his heart.

 If my blood isn't enough to cover Damian's past, it's not enough for yours either.

Damian was an excellent electrician. He'd left Texas and traveled to Oklahoma for a job. He'd been divorced for a while and had given his heart to the Lord Jesus. Once here, he'd prayed and fasted for three days asking for a godly wife.

Following the fast, Damian's roommate asked, "What did God tell you?"

"He gave me Matthew 6:33, 'But seek first his kingdom and his righteousness, and all these things will be given to you as well."

A SIGN

The first time he attended our church, he saw the sign that we'd posted out front.

"But seek first his kingdom and his righteousness, and all these things will be given to you as well."

He took one look at our sign and recognized it as a message from God.

The first time Scotti met Damian's daughter, Alexa, Scotti jumped in the back seat and read her Max Lucado's book *You are Special.* It too was love at first sight.

It was love at first sight for Ken and me when we met Alexa. Curly blonde hair, blue eyes and personality plus, she captured our hearts the first time we laid eyes on her. Kendi and Brannon had two boys, so Alexa was our first granddaughter. By the end of their first weekend, she was calling us Grandmommy and Granddaddy. She was a perfect fit for our family, and we all adored her.

Scotti and Damian met the first week of August 2001. When Damian told us how he wanted to propose, it brought me to tears.

He told Scotti that he'd made reservations at a nice restaurant, knowing she would dress up. Instead of him picking her up, he asked Scotti to pick him up at the church. That aggravated her a little bit. She expected him to pick her up, but he insisted.

The church was dark, and it had started raining. Our parking lot wasn't paved yet, and she didn't want to get out of the car and tramp through rain and mud to a dark church.

Damian urged her to come inside.

She ran through the mud and rain. Inside, Damian said, "There's a question I've been wanting to ask you."

The curtain was closed across the stage, and we were all hidden behind it. As he brought her into the correct position, we opened the curtain. In addition to all of us, there stood a stunning bouquet of 18 yellow roses.

Standing beside the roses, tears streamed down Scotti's face as Ken sang "18 Yellow Roses" to her.

A ROCKET SCIENTIST

Once they were married, Scotti taught school and Damian worked as an electrician. A brilliant man and a real people person, Damian admitted that he'd always dreamed of becoming an engineer.

The engineering program at OSU takes five years. It takes longer if you work fulltime and go to school parttime. That's what Damian did. He commuted to OSU and graduated with a degree in mechanical and aeronautical engineering.

Today, he works for Boeing, a multinational company that designs, manufactures and sells airplanes, rockets, satellites and missiles worldwide. The Lord kept Scotti waiting for a God-loving, guitar-playing, heart-worshipping rocket scientist.

He was worth the wait. Today, Scotti teaches adults through a company called Public Strategies.

Chapter Eleven

A NEW WAY OF LIFE

"*L*et me be honest," I said, "I'll come to your party, but I don't know if I can drink carrot juice."

One of our friends was hosting a gathering to introduce us to juicing. I had grave reservations, but Ken and I had been on a quest to get healthy ever since a cardiologist had told him he was a heart attack just waiting to happen. In only two months of drastic lifestyle changes, Ken's blood pressure and blood tests had all returned to normal.

As I continued researching healthy way lifestyles, I found a lot of contradictions. One expert said you should only eat real butter. Another said not to eat butter, only margarine. One said to eat meat; another said absolutely zero meat. The conflicts were endless and confusing.

At the juicing party, I was stunned to discover that I liked carrot juice. It was cool and fresh with a smooth, creamy texture. It tasted far sweeter than I would have guessed.

Our friends, John and Pat Ward, were at the Fisher's party, and I noticed that John looked younger and healthier than I'd ever seen him.

"What have you been doing to take care of yourself?" I asked John.

"I started running."

"No, it's more than that!" Ken and I had been running marathons, but neither of us looked as good as John.

"If you really want to know," John said, "there's a cassette you can listen to."

When John's wife, Pat, handed me the cassette, it came with a warning. "You can't eat leftovers, and you can't microwave your food."

The cassette was called *Health Through Nutrition* by Dr. Joel Robbins. What he taught about health and nutrition made more sense than anything I'd researched. In terms of food, he went to Genesis 1:29, suggesting we follow God's original food plan for mankind.

"Then God said, 'I give you every seed-bearing plant on the face of the whole earth and every tree that has fruit with seed in it. They will be yours for food.'"

He recommended a diet of fresh fruit, vegetables, nuts and seeds.

SEVEN PRINCIPLES OF HEALTH

 Life is like an onion. You peel it one layer at a time, and sometimes you weep.

— CARL SANDBURG

Dr. Robbins taught that there were seven components to health, and that all seven were necessary for optimal results.

1. Peace with God and man
2. Adequate rest and sleep
3. Fresh air and sunshine
4. Cleanliness and personal hygiene
5. Exercise
6. Pure water
7. Proper nutrition

Peace with God and man dealt with forgiveness, refusing to hold an offense or bitterness. He also taught that grief drained people of their energy. One form of grief was wishing things were different.

He often quoted Carl Sandburg, "Life is like an onion. You peel it one layer at a time, and sometimes you weep."

He offered a Doctor of Naturopathy program through the College of Natural Health in Tulsa. We went through all his curriculum at home the first time. Then we decided we wanted to do it again in person. For the next two years, we drove to Tulsa twice a week to attend his classes. In addition to eating fresh fruit, vegetables, nuts and seeds, we became life-long juicers.

Following the coursework, we had to do an internship, shad-owing him as he treated his patients. He did live blood cell testing, taking a pin drop of blood which, he studied under the microscope.

DEATH SENTENCE

When our friend Bob got sick, his wife rushed him to the hospital, only to find that his kidneys had shut down. "Get your affairs in order," he was told.

When Bob continued to grow worse, we urged him to go see Dr. Robbins, which he did. Dr. Robbins said it wasn't just his kidneys shutting down. His liver was shutting down as well. He put Bob on a diet of fresh fruit and vegetables, seeds, nuts and lots of fruit juice.

Bob was well within a matter of weeks. Both his liver and kidneys started working again, and his energy returned. That was in 1997, and he is still healthy and active today.

Ken and I each earned our Doctor of Naturopathy of Natural Health. We remembered that the Lord had told us that Edmond Christian Center wasn't to be just a church. It was to be a place where Christian activities occurred. We launched Edmond Christian Wellness Center. We offered classes, provided food and recipes, conducted live blood cell testing and individual consultations. Some people came for a month, others for a week or even a year.

One young mother came to us suffering horrible rheumatoid arthritis. After eating according to Genesis 1:29, she was able to walk in only two weeks. The correct food, we learned, gives the body everything it needs to repair and replenish itself.

In addition to eating processed foods, the average American consumes 152 pounds of sugar each year.[1] That's equal to three pounds of sugar a week!

Dr. Robbins also recommended eating only 20 percent of our food cooked. The other 80 percent was to be consumed raw, while the enzymes were still available to our bodies for energy.

Our first real test case involved lifestyle changes for a 15-year-old girl. She was on five different medications for depression and insomnia. A little over five feet tall, she weighed 170 pounds. Under the supervision of Dr. Robbins, she stopped all caffeine, sugar, salt, meat, dairy, additives and preservatives. Within a matter of weeks, she was off all medications.

She ate raw fresh fruits and vegetables, as well as drinking only fresh juices and water. By the end of the school year at Edmond Christian Academy, she weighed 115 pounds, was medication free, alert, productive, active and an honor student. Her depression was a thing of the past.

A mother of eight who went through our program told us, "I've lost 40 pounds, but even more importantly, I've lost self-doubt, worry, headaches, backaches, throbbing teeth and various other complaints."

One after another, people came to the wellness center and found a new lease on life.

During those same years, we enrolled in a correspondence course through Faith Tech Bible College out of Flint, Michigan. From that we started Edmond Christian Center Bible College, using their curriculum. The first night we had 96 students.

SMELL OF DEATH

We went to India with the staff of Faith Tech Bible College in 1996. We taught a group of young men studying to become pastors. Sebastian, a young man in a group of students, asked if we would come and pray for his brother who'd been in a horrible accident. Sebastian was the only member of his family who was a Christian.

Burning smoke and strong spices couldn't mask the unmistakable smell as we walked up the steps in sweltering heat. As we approached Sebastian's brother, the stench of death took our breath away. The accident had crushed his legs. They were so mangled that they didn't even resemble legs. The heat seemed to putrefy his rotting flesh, making us feel queasy.

How do you have faith for this? I thought. I'd never seen anything like it. It was the type of situation where you *had* to pray in faith, because there wasn't a shred of natural hope.

None.

Thanks to God, we knew nothing was impossible for Him.

And that was a good thing, because this was going to require nothing less than a miracle.

Ken laid hands on the young man and prayed God's Word over the situation, commanding healing and restoration. We had no idea what happened after we left.

The heat was oppressive, but the hearts of the people were so precious that we fell in love with them. When we left, the staff asked us not to share our contact information with the students. Later, we discovered that the students had been asked the same thing.

Ten years went by with no contact from anyone in India. Then one day the phone rang at ECA and I heard someone say, "Is this Ken and Bea?"

It was one of our students from India, asking us to come back!

"Moorthi, how did you find us?" I asked.

He'd searched for us on the internet.

We made immediate plans to return to India. When we arrived, each of those young men we'd taught in 1996 were now pastoring churches of their own.

When we arrived, Sebastian said, "My family wants you to come!"

When we arrived at his home, Sebastian's brother *ran* and threw himself in our arms. Those mangled and crushed legs were *whole*. Sebastian's brother and the entire family had given their hearts to Jesus.

What a miracle worker!

Jesus was a miracle worker when He walked on earth in a man's body.

He is still a miracle worker when He walks on earth today in your body and mine.

The people in India received God's Word with great revelation and fresh faith. During one of our trips, Ken taught from Matthew 27:51-53:

"At that moment the curtain of the temple was torn in two from top to bottom. The earth shook, the rocks split and the tombs broke open. The bodies of many holy people who had died were raised to life. They came out of the tombs after Jesus' resurrection and went into the holy city and appeared to many people" (NIV).

That scripture caused a great stir in the class. They turned and talked among themselves. Finally, one of them asked the question they were all wondering about:

"May we teach this boldly?"

"Yes, you may."

They took God's Word to heart, witnessing, praying and seeing miracles performed.

In 2006, we started the Chennai Christian Bible College in Chennai, India. They always wait for us to arrive before holding graduation services, so that we receive the honor of helping confer their degrees. Each time we return, we see the Church in India growing, adding churches, orphanages and local outreaches.

Chapter Twelve

GROWING PROGRAMS AND GROWING FAMILY

ears streamed down my face as I watched the children dance in Katha Bardel's latest performance. I couldn't help myself; it always made me cry. An amazing dance teacher, Katha always chose beautiful Christian music with a message. She choreographed dances that told the gospel story and represented Christian life. How she coaxed such performances out of the children, I'd never know.

Katha's dance company A.R.T.S., stood for Arts Revealing the Son. What an incredible ministry. Kendi and Scotti had taken dance from her for years. Now a whole new generation had the privilege of experiencing that same anointing.

When Katha retired and moved away, her twin daughters picked up the mantle and carried on. In 1988, Katha came out of retirement and moved back to Oklahoma.

"We'll build you a dance studio here on our property if you'll teach these kids," Ken and I told her.

Katha agreed, and we built the studio.

A.R.T.S. was under the covering of Edmond Christian Center, which was more often referred to as ECC. One night, Katha had a dream. She watched a musical dance set to the music of The Nutcracker played out before her. Hers had a different story line and different choreography.

The story in Katha's dream centered around conflicts in Christian families. "It's called *The Prince*," Katha said when she described it to us. "I want to produce it and perform it at ECC."

"We don't have a stage, lights, costumes or the funds to get them," we said. "But we'll pray for God to provide it."

God answered and met all of Katha's needs.

The Lord had impressed Ken, me and Katha that it was to be dinner theater. Our congregation included some incredible cooks. They prepared and served meals to 100 people at each performance. Seated at tables topped with beautiful arrangements and stunning dinnerware.

The Prince opened just after Thanksgiving the year my mother died. Losing her, finding a place for my dad to live, getting him moved and preparing their house to sell had taken a toll. It left me drained and exhausted. Although I never took medicine, I took two ibuprofens that week.

The show opened to rave reviews. I stood in the shadows and wept with gratitude to God for giving Katha the dream and the talent to turn it into a life-changing experience. After a few years, we switched from a dinner theatre to regular seating so that more people would be able to experience it.

MORE GROWTH

Also, under the cover of Edmond Christian Center (ECC), Scotti offered a program called RX, for Reading Experts. She held reading clinics, teaching countless children to read.

Damian wanted to teach karate at ECC. We had reservations about it. We'd show him a book on why Christians shouldn't teach or take karate. He'd show us one on why they should.

He was passionate about the subject and refused to give up. After prayer, we decided to let him teach a class that we would attend. While his students learned the physical movements of a martial art, Damian's focus was on character. For kids to be allowed to continue taking his classes, they had to demonstrate good character and maintain their grades.

"You can't get mad and use this on some kid," he warned them.

Damian prayed with his students, and they studied scripture together. After taking his classes, we had no more reservations. It was a wonderful workout, both physically and mentally. Elite Martial Arts came under the cover of ECC. He was an excellent role model. He also taught Elite Personal Training, circuit training and boot camps.

In 2008, Katha asked us to pray for a young man named Jeff Lewis. We didn't know Jeff, but Katha shared with us that he was a Christian and a very gifted professional dancer, his influence both national and international.

Jeff and his wife, Lisa, had eight children and lived in Houston. While Jeff was dancing in Israel, Lisa died in a tragic accident. He flew home, a widower, to eight broken-hearted children.

We prayed for him and for his children.

DIVINE CONNECTIONS

In February, Jeff came to our campus to lead a dance seminar for ARTS. Ken, Jeff and I met, and there was an instant connection. We felt as though we'd known each other for years.

 I believe the Lord wants me to start a dance ministry called Arrows International. It's supposed to be under ECC.

— JEFF LEWIS

A couple of months later, a mutual acquaintance told me that Jeff was considering putting his children in our school. "Have him call us," I said.

In May, Jeff called. "I really feel like we're supposed to get out of Houston," he said. "I have a lot of interviews over the summer with megachurches. If the Lord doesn't tell me to take one of them, I'll consider coming to Oklahoma."

Jeff's former secretary told him the Lord had shown her the place where He was sending Jeff. She drew a picture of it. It was a red building on a curving road with a man on a tractor in the field behind it.

Throughout the summer, Jeff went for one interview after another. Each time the Lord said, "No."

In late July, he arrived in Edmond. He noticed the way Western Avenue curved near our place. He noticed that our building was red. Then he saw Ken on the tractor and knew he was home.

"We'll need a place to live," Jeff said.

We moved a family out of one of the houses we owned near the school and fixed it up for Jeff and his family. The older four of his children had already graduated high school and were each living on their own. They chose to stay in Houston, which was home to them. Jeff brought the four younger kids with him and enrolled them at Edmond Christian Academy (ECA).

ARROWS INTERNATIONAL

One night Jeff had a dream. He saw the shaft of an arrow hitting a target. "I believe the Lord wants me to start a dance program called Arrows International. It's supposed to be under ECC."

Jeff danced in the studio we'd built for ARTS, who was still under ECC covering but had moved to a larger facility. We built a dormitory for the dance and karate students.

Jeff performed with Project Dance. He'd been praying for Natalie, another professional dancer with Project Dance. Natalie was single and believing God for a husband. Jeff had prayed that the Lord would bring Natalie her mate.

After Jeff's wife's passing, some friends talked about Jeff and Natalie getting together. Neither of them was interested.

God, however, had a different idea.

They were performing together in New York City when Jeff realized that he was the husband that Natalie had been praying for. He proposed, and she accepted.

After a stunning wedding in the gorgeous, glass Thorncrown Chapel in Eureka Springs, Arkansas, Jeff's youngest daughter Mateah, who was six, beamed with delight. "Now I'll have a mommy!" she said.

Natalie was a dream come true for all of us. Not every young woman would marry a man with eight kids, but she settled into life here as though she'd been born for it. In addition to dancing, they each taught at the school. Jeff coached, and Natalie taught Bible.

They felt more like family than friends.

DREAM HOME

The smell of sawdust greeted me at the door of our dream house that was still under construction. After moving so many times, I knew everything that I wanted in this house. We were getting it just the way I wanted it. I walked from room to room, planning out the placement of our furniture in my mind's eye. In the back of my mind, I realized that we were going to need more money than we'd anticipated at the start.

The first part of the answer came when the man who was pouring our concrete asked to buy our mobile home. We'd put a lot of work into fixing it up, so we sold it to him for $10,000. Afterwards, we'd decided to sell the lot too. Ken and I prayed asking God who He wanted to have the land.

A man who lived next door to ECA stopped by and said, "I'm looking for land in the country."

"I'll sell you ours for $10,000," Ken told him.

"I'll take it."

Ken felt bad about the price. "I have to be honest with you," he said. "I bought the land from a sheriff's sale for $900."

"That's great!" the man replied. "That means I have a nice clean title."

All told, we ended up receiving $20,000 on our investment of $3,900. We never felt bad about it because that land is worth a lot of money today.

Once our dream home was finished, Ken, Scotti and I moved in. Within a year or two, Kendi and Brannon moved into their new house next door. We loved having them so close.

The entire time we lived in that house, I continued to be amazed at how right it was for us. "I just love this house!" I said over and over. "It's everything I ever wanted."

That house more than made up for all the years I'd lived in houses while we remodeled. It was a dream come true. Years later, in 2011, Kendi and Brannon decided to move. One Sunday morning at church Kendi said, "Mom, we listed our house with a realtor, and we're having an open house this afternoon. You might as well put a For Sale by Owner sign in your yard and see what happens."

ANOTHER PLACE TO LIVE

We hadn't planned on staying there after Kendi and Brannon moved, so when we got home from church that morning, we put a For Sale sign in our front yard.

Thirty minutes later it sold.

Ken walked next door. "Did you sell your house yet?"

"No."

"We just sold ours!"

The minute the prospective buyers walked into our house, they realized that a lot of thought and prayer had gone into building it. She wasn't leaving without a contract.

Now we had a contract on our house and no idea where to live. We made it a matter of prayer, knowing God must have a plan.

In January, God had spoken the word *simplify* to us. We had no idea where He was leading us. But God! Now we had one less home and yard to care for.

"You know," Ken said, "God often shows you direction through your dreams. Think back to the last one. Part of it hasn't been fulfilled. You dreamed that we were living in an apartment on the second floor of the school. I think that's what we're supposed to do."

The moment he said it, I knew he was right. The second floor of the school had plenty of unused space. We designed our one-bedroom apartment and built it. The move was a huge downsize, but I enjoyed the smaller space, and we felt at home as soon as we moved in. Besides, it was impossible to get a better commute to work.

WORK HARD AND PLAY HARD

As the years passed and the number of programs under the banner of ECC grew, so did our family. Kendi and Brannon had given us three grandchildren. Kenny, our first, was born in

1997. Preston came along in 2001. Evie was added to the family in 2005.

Scotti and Damian brought us Alexa, who fit into the family like a missing piece of a puzzle. Kezia joined us in 2008. Charis made her appearance in 2011.

Each of them was a delight for Ken and me. One of the best things about living on one salary was how much it paid off in the long run. Without incurring any debt, we had always saved and invested anything else we brought in. That meant it was no problem to pay cash for family vacations. They started when Kendi and Scotti were small.

The girls were 14 and six the first time we took them to Disneyland. Mike joined us for the trip. He drove all night so that we arrived at the Grand Canyon at sunrise. The morning sun lit the canyon in pastels. We stood at the overlook in awe at the towering peaks and valleys in the sweeping vista. The Colorado River looked like a ribbon in the distance, its trickling water glistening in the sunlight.

We visited Las Vegas, then continued to Disneyland, where the girls gasped with delight. While in California, we visited my Aunt Gracie in Pasadena. The night before the Rose Bowl, we stood on catwalks and watched the floats come alive for the parade.

We ended up visiting both Disneyland and Disney World many times over the years. We also took a fishing trip to Canada. As the family grew, we took our daughters, sons-in-law and whichever grandchildren were born at the time to visit places all over the world.

We took the family to London, Italy, Greece, Paris, Wales, Ireland, Turkey, China, Alaska and Hawaii. We traveled to Europe several times.

We visited Israel three times and took 12 cruises. Kendi, Alexa, Kenny and Preston all went to India. Kenny, Preston, Leona (my mother-in-law), Mike, my sister May, my sister Fran and her husband, Jack, all went with us on river cruises.

While we always worked hard, we balanced our work life with lots of family fun. It was a decision we never regretted.

Chapter Thirteen

A NEW ADDRESS

*A*ugust 10, 2013, dawned like any other summer morning, hot with clear skies. We always woke early, but when I opened my eyes at 5:30 a.m., Ken was already dressed, standing by the bed. I sat up, blinking the sleep from my eyes.

"I think you need to take me to the Heart Hospital," he said in the same peaceful way that he might ask for a banana in his breakfast smoothie.

I was surprised. He didn't act sick or seem to be in any pain. Besides, we'd managed our health without hospitals most of our married lives.

"Honey, are you sure?"

"I think you need to take me to the Heart Hospital," he repeated.

I dressed in about two minutes, and we arrived at the Oklahoma Heart Hospital at around 6:00 a.m. I dropped Ken off next to the emergency room entrance. He walked inside while I went to park. I followed just a minute or two behind him.

I found him talking to a receptionist. A minute later, Ken was taken back to an exam room.

"Can I go with my husband?" I asked the woman at the front desk.

"Sure, go on back."

"Don't you need me to fill out paperwork?"

"We can do that later. Just go."

Ken lay on an exam table, a cardiologist and a nurse beside him. The nurse checked his blood pressure. "It's high," the doctor said. "Let me give you something to get it down."

He stood next to the bed and watched as the nurse connected the leads to Ken's chest and started an EKG. "Your heart looks good," the doctor said, checking the readouts. As long as you're here, let's run some more tests."

"Which arm would you like me to use?" the nurse asked, pulling out a tourniquet.

Ken didn't answer.

"Honey, she asked you a question," I said, patting him on the arm.

He still didn't respond, which was odd.

"Repeat the EKG," the doctor said.

The leads were still attached, so she ran it again.

CROSSING OVER

"He's had a massive coronary!" The doctor's voice sounded surprised. Turning to me, he said, "You're going to have to leave the room."

I stepped out of the exam room. What was happening? A minute ago, he'd been answering questions with a lazy smile on his face. Then he just seemed to nod off.

Except that he wasn't asleep. He'd slipped gently from the earth realm into eternity within a beat of his heart. I'd seen it on the EKG, beating steady and strong. It didn't slow down. It didn't act up with a strange rhythm.

It just stopped. A beat…then *nothing*. Except eternity.

It reminded me of a biblical term: *The twinkling of an eye.*

That's how things will change when Jesus returns. But that was also the best way to describe what happened to Ken while a doctor, nurse and I watched, unaware.

He changed in the twinkling of an eye—or the beat of a heart.

Was it our age? In the past year, we'd had 15 friends lose their spouses. One of them was healthy and hadn't been under the recent care of a physician. Their house became a crime scene as investigators checked for any sign of foul play.

 "He's not responding," he said. "We'll work on him as long as you want us to, but there's nothing more that we can do."

Just 10 days earlier, my 30-year-old nephew had died. The Oklahoma County Coroner was already behind by 1,000

cases. My nephew's body hadn't been released for a funeral until the coroner could get caught up.

I had no medical training, but it didn't take a medical degree to understand that I'd witnessed Ken have a massive coronary. I was beside him when he died, and they were trying to resuscitate him. Yet, I felt the kind of peace that passes all understanding.

A chaplain came to minister to me. "What happens now?" I asked.

"They'll call the coroner."

I thought of my nephew.

NOTHING MORE TO DO

The cardiologist stepped out to talk to me. "He's not responding," he said. "We'll work on him as long as you want us to, but honestly there's really nothing more we can do."

"If he's gone, he's in heaven," I said. "You don't have to do any more."

"I'm so blessed to hear you say that."

"So, you'll call the coroner?" the chaplain asked.

"No, I was with him when he died," the doctor said. "I'll just sign the death certificate. There's no question, he died of a massive coronary."

They left, and I was glad to have a few minutes to myself. Glad that I had time to process my emotions. I knew the one I loved most on earth had entered his eternal reward with the One we both loved first. Joy flooded my innermost being. Unspeakable joy flooded my heart and soul.

I couldn't imagine life without the love of my life. I didn't want to think about an empty bed, an empty chair, so many empty places. The ripple effect of his death included his daughters never hearing him sing to them again. It meant no wise counsel for Brannon and Damian. It meant no granddaddy there for Alexa, Kenny, Preston, Evie, Kezia and Charis.

It created a huge loss for our congregation. For Jeff and Natalie. For our students. For hundreds of people across the country who knew and loved him. For many people who would mourn him in India.

And yet, I was happy for my sweet Ken. I knew that he was in heaven, and nothing on earth—not even the kids and me—could entice him to come back. He loved us well, but he always loved Jesus most.

LIFE WITHOUT REGRETS

He was only 68, but that was a lot longer than his father had lived. We hadn't lived in fear, but we'd known that Ken had a genetic propensity for heart disease. We'd taken a stand on God's Word. We'd exercised. We'd eaten whole, healthy food with good nutrition. The additional years had provided him with a good quality of life.

We never let the work of the ministry be *work*. We knew that the Bible promised that God's yoke is easy and His burden is light. We believed that and made every day of our lives a day of happiness, gratitude and fun.

I felt enveloped in joy and peace, even when I called Kendi and Scotti. They arrived as peaceful as I was.

"He loved us well," we all agreed, holding one another.

We sat and talked about all the years we'd had him, and realized we agreed on one other thing.

We had no regrets.

We had loved him well, too.

A life without regrets is a wonderful gift from God.

NO SECOND GUESSING

The cardiologist talked to me before we left. "Don't ever second guess yourself," he said. "He was here at the hospital with the best equipment around. I was standing beside him as he passed. You did everything that could possibly have been done. We did everything that we could have."

It wasn't until later that I realized it had been God telling Ken to get to the heart hospital. Had he not been there, it would have taken a long time to get help. This way, I never had to second guess myself.

In addition, because Ken hadn't been sick and under a doctor's care, if we had been at home, the school would have become a crime scene. That was a stressor that none of us needed.

Kendi and Scotti realized our little church building wouldn't hold all the people who would come to celebrate Ken's life. Life Church agreed to let us hold Ken's memorial service at their Oklahoma City location.

Instead of having one person officiate, many people spoke.
People like Scotti and Damian. Jeff Lewis, Hilliard Shackford,
Ben Potter, Jerry Matheson, Rickey Musgrove and others
who'd impacted our lives. Scotti's friend Stacy sang while
Kenny accompanied her on the piano. It was a beautiful
homegoing. I would have enjoyed it so much if Ken had been
at my side.

Kendi ended the service. Here's what she said:

"Growing up, I was the luckiest little girl in the whole
wide world. I know my mom wouldn't approve of the
word lucky, because of course I mean blessed. But
man, looking back on it all, hearing all your stories, it
seems more like luck because I see just how one-in-a-
million my life has been because of my dad.

"Because of how my dad loved me, I grew up knowing
that the one true God of the universe loves me. When
he took me to church every time the doors were open, I
not only learned the song "Jesus Loves Me," but I
believed it was true. When I knocked my front teeth
out, my dad raced me to the hospital in his Beetle with
my head in his lap, I looked up at his face and understood how deeply it pains God to see me hurt.

"When Dad brushed my hair so gently that it never
tugged, I believed that God knows the number of the
hairs on my head and cherishes each one. When I
opened the lunch that he'd packed for me and read the
love notes he'd write on napkins, I knew beyond the
shadow of a doubt that God would provide my every
need. When he promised me as a little girl in French

class that he would make sure I went to Paris, I knew God makes promises that He never breaks, even when it took until my sister's 21st birthday for me to go.

"When he drove me all over the eastern U.S. in his shiny red van, I knew God could be trusted to live out a great adventure, even when I didn't know where all it would take me. When he let me hold the Rand McNally Atlas and navigate alongside him, I learned that God is willing to use every life situation as a learning opportunity to trust Him more.

"When I worked at his side selling hot dogs at his cart downtown, when I read scripture about living in the shadow of His mighty wings, I knew just what that felt like. When he let me ride on top of his briefcase in the middle of the bench seat of his blue Chevy pickup so I could lean on onto my 'big muscle daddy's' right arm, I knew that my God was never too big and strong and powerful or too busy to listen to me when I pray.

"The only time I ever got in big enough trouble that he had to spank me (because my mom wasn't home to do it, not because I never got in trouble), instead my dad decided to show me the power of God's undeserved grace by spanking himself with his own belt while I watched in speechless awe.

"And for the rest of my life, every time I hear old songs like 'Kisses Sweeter Than Wine,' or 'Running Bear and Little White Dove,' or 'Wolverton Mountain,' or 'Eighteen Yellow Roses'—I'll have no trouble picturing God rejoicing over me with singing, just like the Bible says

He does. Because of how deep my father's love for me was, my heart is sure that God is who He says He is, and I am who the Bible says I am.

"Brannon and a few of you laugh at me when I say I'm pretty sure I'm God's favorite. I'm convinced of all of this because of my dad. He was to me and my sister everything an earthly dad could model for us who our heavenly Dad really is. That's just a priceless treasure: to have a father on earth who would love me like that. And as great as that has been, it's not just me and my sister who got to benefit from that love. He loved me really well. But as I look across this room at all your faces, I can see that he loved each of you really well, too.

"So, I want to talk to two groups of people in this room. First, I want to challenge every single one of us who has chosen to submit our hearts fully to Jesus Christ as our Master and Savior and allow God's love to change us from the inside out.

"Because not just you who are daddies to little girls, but every one of us who has that same powerful love living inside of us can do just what my dad did. In First Corinthians 11:1, Paul invites us to follow his example of Christ. Everyone in this room who has surrendered their life to Christ can follow my dad's example. We can love others in a way that shows the whole world just how precious they are to their Father.

"All these funny stories about who my dad was are incomplete without one key piece. His life verse, painted right up on the side of his school and church, is Matthew 6:33. 'Seek God first, and advance His kingdom, and all of these other things will be given to you as well.'

"You can see a life in my dad that may seem unattainable because of all these things he had going for him. But all these things came as a result of him seeking God first. He didn't just believe in God. He let God lead every single aspect of his life. He even put Matthew 6-3-3 at the end of his phone number.

"Don't just think fondly of him. Let his memory challenge you to love harder. Walk out of these doors and live a life that will bring as much glory to God as my dad surely did through his. No offense, but none of you except Scotti had as good a dad as I did. I've been given a great advantage of knowing God as closely as I do. But that doesn't mean that you can't know God as personally, as intimately, and as fully as I have come to know Him.

"There's a second group of you sitting here today who wish you knew the same love of your heavenly Father that I do. Like my dad did. And maybe you want to know for sure you'll meet my dad again someday. You can know, just as surely as I know that my daddy, Ken Sprouse, loved me, that God loves you just as dearly. You can leave with the same peace, joy and hope that's carried my family through these days. That hope is not some intangible feeling. That hope is a person. His name is Jesus Christ.

"It would be my greatest joy to know that my dad's life has been a part of drawing you toward Jesus. We're going to sing one more song before we go, but first, I'd like the chance to pray with those of you who would like to know God like my dad did, like I do. So, if everyone would bow your heads, I'd like those of you who are in this second group to lift your head and look me in the eye.

"Now, let's all pray together with those who will now join us, and my dad, in a very happy reunion on that day when our Lord returns for us.

"Dear Father in heaven, I realize I haven't lived my life for you. I know that I've disobeyed you. I don't want to sin anymore. Thank you for sending Jesus to take the punishment for my sin and make me right with God. Thank you for loving me enough to pursue me here today. I want to know you. I choose to put you first in every area of my life. I give Jesus Christ my whole life. I submit to Him as my Savior. Help me live fully for you until we meet face-to-face. I put my faith in Jesus, and it's in His name that I pray. Amen."

We buried Ken in the Walters Cemetery near his dad. I rode back with Mike and received a text from our dear friend Vickie Fisher.

> I'll be your secretary, cook, custodian or all the above.

True to her word, she walked with me until 2017 when we sold the school property.

Throughout the days and weeks that followed, many people asked when I would close the church and the school. The answer was, *Never, until God tells me to do it.* Events don't direct my life. That's the job of the Holy Spirit.

"Surely, you're not going to live here alone? Aren't you afraid?"

"No, I'm not afraid. We've been here 15 years. This is home."

The day he made his transition, I said, "Lord, I can't do everything Ken and I did together. Show me what I *can* do and send the people to do the rest."

He did just that, surrounding me with people who helped.

The church and the school continued, although everything seemed more of a struggle without Ken beside me. Learning to live without him was like learning to live without my heart. It was only possible through Christ.

GOD'S FINGERPRINTS

Looking back, I saw a pattern of events that appeared different in hindsight. For instance, God gave us a lot of our direction through my dreams. The last time I'd had a dream of significant direction, I'd described it to Ken.

Ken pondered it and then said, "I don't think I'm in that dream."

"Of course, you are!" I insisted.

Later, I went back and reviewed the details of the dream.

Ken wasn't in it.

I felt shocked. What did that mean?

It's clear to me now that God had used that dream to show us both that I had a future that didn't include Ken.

The other thing I noticed was that in the year leading up to his death, God honored Ken in unusual ways. It was as though God was celebrating Ken's life early, before he passed.

For instance, Kendi and Scotti adored our love story. Instead of waiting to celebrate our 50th wedding anniversary, they got the idea to celebrate the 50th anniversary of the day we met.

As part of that celebration, we had new family photographs made. A friend of Kendi's, Grant Downing, interviewed Ken and me separately, asking us each the same questions. Then they put together a video of each of us answering the questions. Grant created an amazing, hilarious video, showing each of us answering the questions. The video also featured old photos, old home movies and romantic music from our era. They celebrated that milestone in January of 2013. Ken died that August. If they'd waited for our 50th wedding anniversary, he wouldn't have been here. (To see the video, go to YouTube and search for Ken & Bea – 50 years!)

That year, we celebrated Ken's 50th reunion from Walters High School. Then in May, we took the Sound of Music Tour and Viking River Cruise. We traveled with Mike, Ken's sister Chris and her husband Joel and our grandson, Preston. We had a carefree and fun time with Ken.

After returning from Europe, Mike, Ken and I went to Branson, Missouri and while there got a call that Mike's mother had passed away in Arizona.

We'd been partners with Kenneth Copeland Ministries for many years. But that year, 2013, our story was featured in the April issue of their magazine, the *Believer's Voice of Victory.* Not only was our story in the magazine, but our photograph was even on the cover.

Only God could have orchestrated Ken being honored in such powerful ways while he was still alive.

As I learned to live without Ken, I leaned more on the Lord for comfort and support. A special time for us as educators had always been spring break. I noticed that God made sure to see that I had plans over that first spring break without Ken to keep my mind occupied. Day by day and month after month, Jesus became more of my Rock than ever before. I missed Ken, but I was never alone.

During Edmond Christian Academy's Spring graduation, our first two grandchildren received their diplomas without Ken. Before he left this earth, Ken had planned and paid for their Senior Trip to Europe. We all celebrated what would have been Ken's 69th birthday in Paris. Kenny, our eldest grandson, said, "I'll bet the celebrations are even better than this in heaven."

Chapter Fourteen

A CHANGE OF PLANS

The praise and worship music at Life Church drew me into the sanctuary the first Saturday evening after Ken's memorial service. The kids didn't want me to sit home alone on Saturday night and encouraged me to go to Life Church with them. Since our little church met on Sunday, there was no conflict.

"You know, I love coming here and getting filled up without any responsibility," I told my daughters, "It's like a spiritual shot in the arm." Visiting Life Church blessed me so much that I continued going on Saturday evenings. I often attended multiple services, inviting friends to join me.

After a while, Kendi said, "Mom, you need to serve with us."

I knew that was wise advice. I started volunteering to teach the children at the 4:00 service Saturday afternoon. Then I sat and enjoyed the 5:30 service with my family.

The week before Christmas in 2016, there were 11 services, and I had volunteered to help at all of them. On Wednesday, the woman in charge of volunteers said, "You volunteered for *all* the services. Don't you want to listen to the Christmas message at least once?"

"Only if there are enough volunteers," I said, knowing that a lot of people were out of town for the holidays.

On Wednesday evening, December 21, there were enough volunteers for the kids rooms, so I sat and listened to Craig Groeshel's message. In my life, I'd heard a lot of powerful messages, but I'd never heard a better Christmas message. In short, the message said that we each have a plan for our lives. But God has a higher purpose, and sometimes that means a change of plans.

I drove home that cold, wintry night, meditating on that sermon. I had the strongest sense that God had spoken a personal message to me. I sensed that He had a change of plans for me.

Back home, I sorted through a large stack of mail, tossing most of it into the trash. I always got a lot of mail from other churches, often inviting me to things I didn't have time to attend.

I picked up an envelope from yet another church and paused. I didn't throw it away. In an uncharacteristic move, I opened it and read it.

Then I read it again.

"Would you be interested in selling us your property?"

A NEW DAY

I wouldn't have given that a second thought if I hadn't just heard that sermon and sensed that God had a change of plans for me. Was it time to sell?

I prayed about it and sensed it might be time for me to move ahead with caution.

I called that church the next day, which was the Thursday before Christmas. A group of people came to tour the property. We'd been talking for about 15 minutes when one of them asked, "You keep talking about *we*. Who is *we*?"

"I'm talking about my husband, Ken," I explained. "He went to heaven, but I still talk about him as though he was here. We built all this together."

We walked through the four buildings. They asked me a lot of questions and loved everything. As they were leaving, one of them said, "We feel as though we know Ken."

Another group from the church toured another day.

I talked to my daughters and with the people in our congregation. They all said the same thing, "You've got to hear from God."

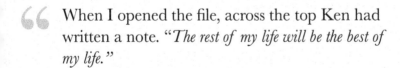 When I opened the file, across the top Ken had written a note. *"The rest of my life will be the best of my life."*

It was Christmas break, so the school was closed. I woke early one morning as usual and heard the voice of the Lord.

"Just like I told you 30 years ago: I wouldn't ask you to do anything that wasn't good for you. Do you realize how much I love you? And I wouldn't ask you to do something that isn't for your good. Turn loose of the trapeze and soar with me. I'll take you to places you've never dreamed of."

LETTING GO

I knew without a doubt, that it was time to let go of everything. It was time to sell the property. It was time for a new phase of my life, soaring with God.

All our grandchildren had attended our school, and some were still enrolled. Not all of them would graduate from ECA. I felt a moment of remorse before remembering how hard it had been to pull Kendi and Scotti out of Casady. But I knew God had plans for my grandchildren too. And I knew I could trust Him with them.

The church buying the property wanted an appraisal. "I do things differently," I said. "I'm not getting an appraisal." I explained that they were welcome to have one done, which they did.

I remembered that a few years before Ken died, someone had offered to buy the school. Ken had figured out what the land with the buildings was worth, as well as all the extra acres we owned adjacent to the property.

I had no idea where that information was, but I searched his files until I found it. When I opened that particular file, across the top Ken had written a note. *"The rest of my life will be the best of my life."*

I felt as though Ken was standing there with his hands on my shoulders. God's message was clear, *Your best is yet to come.*

LIFE IN THE FAITH LANE

The life I'd lived with Ken had been wonderful beyond my expectations. I couldn't imagine how the future could be better than the past.

But I knew it was true.

Inside the file, Ken had mapped out all the data. He had listed the value of the land and buildings and the additional acres. His appraisal had been done in 2008. Now, in 2016, it was outdated. I felt as though I was to sell it for them for the price of Ken's appraisal. They agreed to purchase the land and buildings. I kept the extra acres.

ARROWS

One part of our discussion was about Arrows International. They still needed access to the studio and the dormitory.

"Right now, we have no need for those buildings," they told me. "We'd be delighted for Arrows International to continue using them until we do. When that happens, we'll give you a year's notice."

We all breathed a sigh of relief that Arrows wouldn't have to relocate now.

I prepared the daunting task of closing the school. One of the hardest things I was facing was emptying Ken's office. Thanks to good friends from Missouri, Eldon and Lynn Craig, that had already been done.

Two years earlier, my friend Lynn Craig and I'd gone through all of Ken's handwritten sermon notes and cassette tapes.

How could I get rid of them?

"You have them in your heart," she assured me. "That's where they were meant to be. You're living them. You don't need a hard copy."

I knew she was right, and the girls agreed.

"What I've found," Lynn said, "is that whatever you don't deal with now, you'll just have to deal with later. The stuff we hang onto is temporal. What we carry inside us is the eternal part."

That piece of wisdom was so liberating.

SO MANY CHANGES

We'd been planning a 30-year anniversary of the school for this year, even before Ken went to heaven. Now I realized that the anniversary celebration would also coincide with the school's closing. This would be our last graduating class. It felt surreal.

Ken's cousin Mike joked with me, "Bea, you're going to be homeless."

With a start, I realized that I'd never bought a house that Ken hadn't walked through. I'd never bought a house without him. This would be another of those stretching experiences.

I couldn't start looking for a place to live because I'd booked a cruise. The very day we came home from the cruise in mid-February, the girls and I started looking at houses.

I knew two things about my future home. I didn't want a big house to clean and keep up with. And I'd always thought it would be fun to live in a cute little house on Boulevard Avenue near downtown Edmond.

The day we got home from the cruise, there was an open house on Boulevard. When I arrived, Kendi was just leaving. "Mom, you're not going to like it."

She knew me well.

I was looking at a patio home when Kendi called. "Come see this house!" she said. "You're going to love it!"

She was right again. I loved everything, except the shower.

I went to my exercise class, and while I was there, Kendi sent me a text.

> Are you going to buy that house?

> Not today! I don't like the shower and I just started looking.

> If you're not going to buy it, we are.

Brannon and Kendi fell in love with the house and bought it. I was thrilled for them.

A NEW HOME

A week or so later, I saw a house for rent on Boulevard. It was cute and appeared to have been updated. I called and made an appointment to see it.

The moment I stepped inside I said, "Would you be willing to sell it?"

"Well, we bought it to rent," the owner said. "But I'll talk to my wife."

Two days later, he called and agreed to sell it to me.

We closed on March 19, 2017.

Ken and I had bought our furniture 50 years earlier, which I still loved. I had some of the boys from the school move it to my new house.

It was too big!

"Boys," I said, "this is practice for marriage. I need you to move the furniture back."

This was a new season of my life, and it included a new look.

We were preparing for the estate sale, the last graduation and the 30-year anniversary. People were coming from across the nation to celebrate with us. I had everything organized, down to the food trucks. We'd invited a lot of the former teachers and students to speak.

My only disappointment was that Mike, who now lived in Arizona, couldn't be with us. He'd been such an integral part of our lives that it was a real disappointment that he couldn't make it.

On Friday afternoon, before the celebration on Saturday evening, I stood on my front porch polishing the glass on my front door. I watched a red car pull into my driveway. I couldn't see who it was through the car's tinted windows.

Mike leapt out of the car and flung his arms out. "Surprise!"

Having Mike there gave my heart a jolt of happiness.

THE POWER OF INTEGRITY

Charles Jones arrived from Nashville. I still remembered the day we met him. It had been back in the 70s when the school was in a rental property on Second Street. Ken looked outside and saw a man standing in the parking lot.

"I'd like to meet Ken Sprouse," the man said when Ken walked out to greet him.

"Here I am," Ken said, holding out his hand.

"I own properties all over the country," Charles explained. "You're the only man who always pays me on time or early. It's a pleasure to meet you."

Integrity. That's what drew Charles to meet Ken that day. You just didn't meet many people with the kind of integrity that Ken lived by. Charles Jones was also a man of great integrity. That began a lifelong friendship.

On Saturday, the day of the celebration, a group of us attended the Edmond Arts Festival and had a great time. That evening, the entire celebration went off without a problem. One nice surprise was that the book we'd put together of some of Ken's teachings had arrived and copies available. The name of the book was *Don't Look Back*.

A MESSAGE FROM GOD

I thought the program was over until Jeff Lewis led me to the front. The graduating class stood on the stage with Jeff and Natalie. They spoke the following things to me.

Sarah: A voice from heaven proclaiming, Don't look back.

Graduating Class: Don't look back.

Jeff: You've activated faith and hope. A hope that won't disappoint. Don't look back.

Graduating Class: Don't look back.

Natalie: You've taught and guided so many. Don't look back.

Graduating Class: Don't look back.

Mateah: You've shown grace and mercy. Don't look back.

Graduating Class: Don't look back.

Coller: You've stirred laughter and tears. Don't look back.

Graduating Class: Don't look back.

Cody: You've expressed forgiveness and hope. Don't look back.

Graduating Class: Don't look back.

Searra: You have a heart of praise and a humble spirit. Don't look back.

Graduating Class: Don't look back.

Sarah: You are a reflection of God's love. Don't look back.

Graduating Class: Don't look back.

Cody: Bea Sprouse

Searra: Your latter days

Collier: Will be greater

Mateah: Than your former days

Graduating Class: Don't look back, Bea Sprouse. Look forward. Step forward.

Jeff and Natalie danced a beautiful tribute to the song *Don't Look Back.*

God couldn't have made His message more clear:

Big changes are coming.
The best is still ahead.
Don't look back.

Chapter Fifteen

A NEW IDENTITY

The seatbelt sign blinked on as the airplane bounced through turbulence. I looked out the window and saw the sun setting over the ocean. Hearing Jeff and Natalie laugh, I looked over at them. One of them had ordered cranberry juice, and the other ordered ginger ale. They'd been pouring it together when a bump of turbulence had caused it to spill.

They laughed, mopping it up.

They reminded me so much of Ken and me. Like cranberry juice and ginger ale, they were better together than they could ever have been apart.

I watched them sip their drinks, oblivious to the turbulence. They'd been asking for years to go with me to India, and we were on our way. But I still wasn't sure how it would all play out.

I'd watched them minister in many places in the U.S. and abroad, but I just couldn't imagine how it would work in India.

The heat was unrelenting. Worse by far than other places where they'd danced. There were constant problems with transportation in India. How would we transport a whole team of dancers from place to place?

There were problems with lodging. Where would they stay?

There were problems with food. Who would prepare and cook it?

This was the first time I'd been to India since Ken died. Jeff and Natalie kept asking to go, so I relented. We didn't bring a team, though. It was just Jeff, Natalie and me, spying out the land.

I'd never been to India without Ken. The first thing I noticed when I got to my room was that the security latch didn't work. I walked back to the front desk and explained the situation. They nodded and smiled but didn't fix it. I went back and reported the problem again. It still wasn't fixed. The third time I reported it, I knew that either they didn't understand what I was saying, or they just weren't going to fix the problem.

I felt so alone and vulnerable.

Standing in my room, I said, "I don't like being here alone!"

I jumped when an *audible* voice echoed through the room.

"You are never alone!"

Peace flooded me, and I knew that I had more protection than a security latch could offer. When Jeff and Natalie heard about the problem, they offered to get me moved to another room. "No, I'm fine," I told them.

And I was. I never thought about the security latch again. I knew that for the rest of my days, it didn't matter where in the world I found myself, I would never be alone.

The trip went better than I could have imagined. The urging in their hearts to minister in India proved to be straight from God's heart. We began planning what it would take to bring a team of dancers.

After returning home, I told that story to one of my friends. I didn't know at the time that her husband had terminal cancer. She told me that she'd been worrying about what she would do when she was alone. The answer of course was that she would never be alone.

No matter what we're facing, we're never, ever alone.

The next time we traveled to India, Jeff, Natalie and I brought a small team of dancers with us. No one in India had seen anything like it. I watched in amazement as the dancers opened door after door for us that had never been opened to us before.

Each time we went back, we took more dancers. In 2018, we took 14. Places in India that I didn't know existed couldn't wait for us to visit them. God used Arrows International to expand our ministry there.

In addition, I realized that God had used Jeff and Natalie to cushion the transition of my traveling to India without Ken.

THE SOUTHERN CROSS

Back in 2013, I'd joined them on a ministry trip to New Zealand. I found myself on New Year's Eve looking up at the Southern Cross. I blinked back tears as I saw the four brightest stars in a small constellation in the Milky Way that formed a cross in the night sky.

Wherever we went, God was faithful to reveal Himself and His plan of redemption to the world through creation. This was yet another perfect example.

Before we left for New Zealand, I kept wondering why I was going. It wasn't about my helping them. I helped, of course, but I didn't do anything that someone else couldn't have done.

Then I realized that I wasn't there to help them. God had me sitting under two weeks of their anointed ministry to heal *my* heart. The Lord used Arrows' anointed dance ministry to restore my soul.

Standing on the beach, looking up at the Southern Cross, was restoring *my* soul. This was all part of God's process for me. That was our God. Always restoring our souls. Especially after a traumatic loss. Jeff and Natalie shared their New Year's hug with me.

Later that year, after returning from New Zealand, the church who'd bought our property gave us notice that was inevitable one day. They would need to start using the studio that served as Arrows' home base within a year.

After praying, I knew Edmond Christian Center needed to build a new facility for them on the acres we still owned on Western Avenue. This would be my first building project without Ken. It seemed harder than any other assignment so far.

In January 2019, the first step in the process involved applying for a building permit. Those were the kinds of details that Ken had always handled.

Could I do it? I felt so far out of my comfort zone.

A REMINDER

The county office where I needed to apply was in downtown. I called to ask what was required. A woman named Markita emailed the information to me. On the bottom of her email, it said, "I know the plans I have for you," Jeremiah 29:11.

Those words leapt off the page and into my heart. God spoke to me through them, assuring me that this had been His plan when He formed me in my mother's womb.

"For I know the plans I have for you," declares the Lord. "Plans to prosper you and not to harm you. Plans to give you hope and a future."

It sounded for a moment like God had shouted those words at me.

They impacted me so much that I wanted to meet Markita. I called her. "I've got a few questions," I said, "will you be in the office all day?"

"Yes, but you don't need to drive downtown. Let's see if I can help you over the phone."

"No, I'll come downtown."

"The parking is a little difficult."

"That's all right. I'll be down today."

When I arrived, Markita was there with two men. "What do I need to get the surveyor to do?"

She asked one of the men. He pulled up a document. "It's all done," he said. He looked at me and said, "It was handled back when you sold the adjoining property. It doesn't need to be redone."

He remembered from the sale of the property! I wondered if he may have been an angel.

Afterwards, everyone left except Markita. "This is my first building project since my husband moved to heaven," I explained. "I wanted to meet you after reading the scripture at the bottom of your email. It said, 'I know the plans I have for you.'"

She leaned forward, her eyes sparkling with joy. "Now you *know* you can do it!"

"That's right." I left knowing that God had given me a word in season.

HE RESTORES MY SOUL

God is always in the business of repairing, restoring and healing us. In Psalm 23, he said, "The LORD is my shepherd, I lack nothing. He makes me lie down in green pastures he leads me beside quiet waters, he refreshes my soul."

Notice that it says God *makes* me lie down so He can refresh my soul. He doesn't *suggest* it. When we were trying to decide where to put the new building, Jeff walked up to the highest hill and looked down over the acres before him. There was the red building. The curving road and the tractor Ken had driven. He looked over the acres where Arrows' new facility would stand. That's when he realized that this was the place where God had brought him for a purpose.

"The first day I got here, Jesus said, 'You're going to be a teacher here in heaven, but first you're going to sit under the teachings of Paul.'

Today is my first day to get to teach."

God made him lie down in these green pastures to restore his soul.

I realized that my little house on Boulevard was a green pasture. It was a cocoon of peace where God was restoring my soul.

A TEACHER IN HEAVEN

Pastor Joel, a longtime friend, had a dream two years after Ken's passing. He said it was so vivid that he didn't know if it was a dream or if he'd gone to heaven in the spirit.

Here's what he saw:

"I saw Ken dressed in white and happier than I'd ever seen him. Over to the side there were about 30 white chairs with people sitting in them. He turned to me and said, 'The first day I got here,' Jesus said, 'You're going to be a teacher here in heaven, but first you're going to sit under the teachings of Paul.'

Today is my first day to get to teach.'"

Pastor Joel's dream took my breath away. Above anything else, Ken loved to teach. He was always one of the happiest people on earth, but he was even happier teaching in heaven. It also sounded like he'd spent the first two years sitting under Paul's teaching.

He must have been breathless with joy over that.

A HOUSE IN HEAVEN

Three years later, Pastor Joel had another vivid dream which he sent to me:

> "Good evening, Ms. Bea! I've been going through some difficult things, and I'm sitting here in front of the fireplace talking to the Lord. Suddenly it was like Ken was here with me! He was always my go-to guy when I needed advice.

> "Then I saw Ken in the spirit. He was dressed in a long, white robe with many different colored linen scarves. He was walking around heaven with Paul. They were talking and talking. Just then, Jesus showed up, and Ken was telling them all about me.

> "Ken turned to me and said, 'Tell Bea, Jesus and I are building her a big ole house! He keeps showing me things about the house that I never dreamed of. We're doing it together!

> "'Don't worry. There was no mistake. It was my time to go. It was all part of the plan. I had to leave for other things to happen. You know what I mean. Don't worry, it will be worth it all when you get here. Keep going! You're doing right. Follow the path.'"

I knew that Ken was happier than he'd ever been. I knew he'd been sending me messages and building me a house. God has been so wonderful to allow me those glimpses into heaven. But the Lord had some other things He wanted to help me with.

THE TRUTH ABOUT MARRIAGE

When people asked if I would ever marry again, I often said, "What would be the odds of me ever finding another man like Ken Sprouse, by which I mean his character and his integrity?"

In May of 2014, not even a year after Ken went to heaven, I was pondering that one day. Scotti, Damian and I were sitting in an upstairs restaurant in Ireland when a bus rumbled by. A banner on the side of the bus read: *No Dream Too Big; No Odds Too High.*

Those words took my breath away.

In London on that same trip, I saw a billboard advertising *Shakespeare in Love*. It said, *Are You Ready to Fall in Love Again?* Of course, I wasn't ready then, but I found it interesting that the Lord seemed to be posing questions like that to me.

Over the next few years, I had the same exact dream on three occasions. Ken was here, and I was so excited I wanted to call the girls and say, "Dad's back!" But there was something odd about the experience. Ken was here, but *not* here. He seemed detached. I knew he still loved us and was checking up on us to see that everything was going well. But it wasn't the same as when he lived on earth.

I expected him to hug me, but he didn't. The dreams aggravated me.

Then I had a different dream. It was very vivid. Ken was here, and he said, "We're not a couple anymore."

"Don't say that!" I insisted.

He walked away and told two other people. "Bea and I aren't a couple anymore."

"Don't say that!" I repeated.

He kept telling people we weren't a couple anymore.

When I woke, I was still frustrated. Like Mary, I began to ponder those things in my heart. I know the Bible says that in heaven we won't marry or be given in marriage. In other words, *we won't be a couple anymore.*

Still, for those of us who have been blessed with wonderful marriages, our human mind pictures us together in eternity.

The Lord was showing me in the most literal sense that we aren't a couple anymore. We will never be a couple again. Not in this dispensation or the next.

Our time on earth to be a couple is over. It will never happen again for all of eternity.

When it comes to heaven, I agree with that fabulous song by Mercy Me: *I Can Only Imagine!* But what I've come to realize is that the love in heaven is about Him. Yes, I'll enjoy hugging Ken and many others that I've loved on earth.

But it won't be about *them.*

The person I'll run to with matchless love is Jesus!

I realized that no matter how wonderful a marriage is here on earth, we must always make sure our mate is in second place. First place always belongs to Jesus.

Chapter Sixteen

A NEW LIFE

*A*fter Ken transitioned to heaven, I joined a group called Grief Share. We all shared our experiences in dealing with the loss of a loved one. Talking to two ladies from the group, I told them that a man in our church was pushing me toward a romantic connection with Ken's cousin, Mike. I explained that Mike and I were just friends.

"Well, you sure light up every time you talk about him," one of them said.

My other friend added, "We're just saying that it appears that there's something there."

I pondered that and realized that I probably knew Mike better than any man other than Ken. Although they were cousins, Ken and Mike behaved more like brothers. They were closer than many brothers I'd known.

They vacationed together. Owned businesses together. Ran marathons together. There was even a short time when Mike lived with us. So we had years of shared history. We understood one another's jokes. We could almost finish one another's sentences.

One of the many things I loved about Ken was his wonderful sense of humor. He managed to find something fun in the most trying times. Which was one of the same things I admired about Mike. Mike was both fun and funny. Everybody loved Mike, all our friends and family.

Which is why Kendi and Scotti warned me not to think about him as husband material. "Mom," they said, "as much fun as Mike is, don't expect your relationship with him to ever change. He never married, and he won't at this late date. He's a confirmed bachelor."

I knew they were right, still I found myself feeling letdown. Then I decided to just be grateful I had him as a friend.

After closing the school in 2017, one of our longtime friends, also a widower, put his hand on mine and said, "I came here with the intention of asking you to marry me."

Although his sudden proposal caught me off guard, I was humbled that a man of his caliber would ask to marry me. This was a man who had as much integrity as Ken. He was in the upper tier of all the men I knew.

He told me that after his wife had died, he reflected on all the Christian women he knew. I was the only one he could imagine marrying. What an incredible honor. He was sound spiritually, mentally, emotionally and financially. I told him I'd pray about it.

Both of my daughters were thrilled. "Not many people would turn down a proposal from him, Mom."

I knew I wasn't in love with him. However, he was such a kind, sweet, gentle and godly man, he would be easy to love. He suggested that we give it a year and see if we fell in love.

Meanwhile, Kendi had scheduled a trip to visit several different Life Church locations across the country. Her trip ended in the city where he lived. We went to church with him and met his daughter. When we got in the car to head home, my son-in-law was on the phone. The whole family wanted to know what I thought.

As easy as he was to love, I knew this man wasn't God's plan for my life. I returned to my little house on Boulevard in Edmond, Oklahoma, alone. It was still my green pasture, the quiet place where God was healing my soul.

THE WHITE FLAG

The following Spring of 2018, I ran across another longtime friend who had also lost his wife. "Would you ever consider remarrying?" he asked.

"I never thought I would," I admitted. "But I've changed my mind. I would for the right person, if it was God's plan."

"Yeah, me too. I always thought I would never remarry. But I've changed my mind. Now I think I would, too." He and I talked for a long time that day.

Although we didn't live in the same town, he started calling me a lot. I was stunned at how much we had to talk about. Deep conversations. We discussed the challenges of putting marriages together at our ages.

During this time, I was looking for a new car. He helped me find one, and even negotiated the deal. "Thank you for helping me find and buy a car!"

"Thank you for trusting me."

I realized that I *did* trust him.

In January of 2020, I took a cruise that featured some bands, including Mercy Me. Afterwards, we resumed talking about the possibility of marriage.

"I guess I'll just put up the white flag of surrender," he said.

Those words gave me pause. I remembered the way Ken loved me.

"That's not good enough for me," I said. "I don't want a surrender. I've got to have someone who can't live without me."

That's what I'd had with Ken, and I wasn't willing to settle for anything less. We decided that marriage was off the table and agreed to just be friends.

A WORD FROM GOD

In 2018, two men of God heard from the Lord that I would marry again. Jeff Lewis had a vision and said, "God's going to bring a man into your life. But there's going to have to be little adjustments made."

I believed those words. Of course, I knew who I would have chosen, but Mike and I had always been in the friend zone. I didn't see any signs of that changing. Besides, we seldom saw one another. He lived in Arizona, and I lived in Oklahoma.

However, I needed to know if there was anything at all in that relationship.

"Father," I prayed, "I need some face-to-face time with Mike so that I can know if our relationship might go any further." I didn't tell anyone about my little prayer.

The next week Mike called. "Hey, what are you going to be doing in October?"

"Why do you ask?"

"I thought I might come visit in either October or at Thanksgiving."

I knew that God had answered my prayer. "Come in October," I said.

Doing what Mike does best, he planned a whole week of fun things to do. We took a guided walk through historic Edmond. We visited a train museum in Enid. The last night he was here, we took a horse-drawn carriage ride, complete with S'mores.

Afterwards, he took me home before heading back to his hotel. Before he left, he kissed me on the cheek! I went inside and squealed. Mike didn't kiss women, even their cheeks. I figured for Mike, a kiss on the cheek was as good as a proposal!

The next morning, he refused to talk about the kiss. After church, he got in his car and drove back to Arizona. Back home, Mike continued doing what he'd done since Ken's death. He sent funny cards, gifts and flowers.

Go figure. I didn't know what that meant, if anything.

UNEXPECTED JOURNEY

In February of 2020, my sister May said, "We want to go to Arizona and have Mike be our tour guide."

Shocked, I looked at my brother-in-law. He shrugged. "I know."

We were surprised because May didn't like traveling that far. "Are you sure you feel like going?"

"I want to get out of town," May said.

"I want to go, but it has to be by February 18," I told them.

I had scheduled another trip to India with Arrows International. That would be cutting it close, but I thought it would work.

I called Mike. "May and Jack want to come to Arizona. And they want you to be their tour guide. But it has to happen by February 18."

"Yes, I'm available."

"We need to find a place to stay."

"Wait a minute!" Mike said. "Are you coming?"

"Yes."

"Then I'm not going to be here." That was typical Mike, and I just laughed.

There was a church in town that Mike listened to and supported financially. However, he'd never attended in person. I'd been trying to get him to attend, but without success.

"We'll arrive on a Wednesday," I explained. "After we get settled, you and I are going to attend that church."

May, Jack and I had a pleasant drive to Arizona. When we arrived, we greeted Mike and then checked into the bed and breakfast. Afterwards, I hopped into Mike's car to go to church.

"You look very inviting."

I was stunned. Mike *never* said anything flirty to anyone.

"Well, thank you, Mike."

We filled out the visitor's cards as Mike Sprouse and Bea Sprouse. I realized that they would probably assume we were married. The pastor stood in the pulpit and wept. If she'd met Mike on the street, she wouldn't have known who he was. But for years, he'd not only listened to the services, but he'd also contributed finances that had made a huge impact on the church. He was embarrassed by her words, but I was glad people glimpsed the man behind the money.

ANOTHER SURPRISE

The next day, Mike took us to see amazing sights. That evening, when we got back to the bed and breakfast, May and Jack went inside. Mike and I sat in the car and talked.

"You are the most fun person in the world to be with," Mike surprised me by saying.

"Thanks, Mike."

"May I kiss you?"

Wait. What??

My heart beat like a jackhammer in my chest.

Mike. Sprouse. Asked. To. Kiss. Me.

Somehow, I managed to get my mouth to work just in time. "Yes."

He kissed me!

The next day was a repeat of the day before. Mike took us sightseeing all day. Then before going home, he said, "You are the most fun person in the world to be with. May I kiss you?"

Of course he could.

"What are you doing after we get back tomorrow night?" he asked.

"I have no plans."

"Maybe we could go get a Coke or something? I'd like to talk to you."

"Okay, that would be fine."

Our final day in Arizona, Mike took us to new places to visit. As usual, we laughed and had a great time. When we dropped May and Jack off at the bed and breakfast, Mike said, "I'll bring Bea back later. I'd like to talk to her."

May and Jack didn't think a thing about it.

Later, he said, "You are the most fun person to be with. We just have to find a way to be together more often."

Then. He. Proposed.

To this day, I don't remember exactly what he said. When my ears heard him, my mind short-circuited. It just fizzled. Fried. Fireworks exploded inside me. Somehow, I must have said yes.

Ken had been gone seven years. It was time.

Later, I asked, "So I get to be Bea Sprouse for the rest of my life?"

"Yes, unless you'd like to hyphenate it. You could be Bea Sprouse-Sprouse." I laughed at the idea.

BIG DECISIONS

I'd always believed a wife should go wherever her husband wanted to go. I couldn't help but wonder what it would be like living in Arizona with Mike and his faithful dog, Scout. I'd never had a dog that lived inside, but I was willing to vacuum every day to be with Mike. Before we could discuss it, he settled the issue.

"We're going to live in Oklahoma. And Scout's not coming in the house."

"Mike, I'm happy to live in Arizona."

"No, we're living in Oklahoma."

May, Jack and I were leaving early the next morning, and I wouldn't see Mike again for a while. As excited as I was to tell them that they'd facilitated Mike's proposal, I thought it only fair to tell my children first.

That created a dilemma. Each of my daughters and sons-in-law had schedules that were crazy busy. As the family had grown, adding in the schedules of all the grandchildren meant we had to work to find a time that everyone was available to get together. I couldn't see it happening before I left for India. We agreed to keep our engagement a secret until I had a chance to tell my kids.

We also discussed my upcoming trip to India. It was already booked, and it was too late to change it. It was also too late for Mike to join us.

"Make me a promise before you go," Mike said. "No matter what happens in India, don't let anything stop you from coming home when you're scheduled." I couldn't imagine anything like that happening, but I promised. Later, that promise would seem prophetic.

That night, Mike sent me a song by Frank Sinatra which I'd never heard. It was called "I Have Dreamed What It Would Be Like To Be Loved By You." I listened to the words over and over all night. He called the next morning before we left, and we compared notes. Neither of us had slept.

On Sunday morning after I returned from Arizona, Scotti called. "I made all this food for Life Group. Now it's been cancelled. Let's see if everyone can come here. We can have an impromptu family meeting," she joked.

Everyone could come!

A sudden, unplanned family meeting? That was as unusual as May deciding she wanted to travel to Arizona. I saw God's fingerprints all over it. I called Mike, and we agreed that I should tell them.

After dinner that evening, the kids were off doing their thing. The adults settled in Scotti's family room. I pulled up a stool and sat so that I could see everyone's faces. There was no way to lead into it.

"Mike and I are getting married."

Their faces registered two things simultaneously.

Shock and pure joy.

"There's no one you could have picked that would have been better for you to marry," Damian said, finding his voice first. Then everyone erupted, talking about it and rejoicing. Then one of the group said, "This is Mike's first marriage. His first wedding. So he should have it however he wants it."

"Mike's probably not going to want anyone there," I warned. That was one difference between Mike and me. I was an extrovert; Mike was an introvert.

"Then that's how it should be," they all agreed. "However he wants it."

That night I called Mike and told him what the kids said. "I told them you probably wouldn't want anyone there."

"You're right, I don't. What do you think about getting married in that glass chapel in Bella Vista, Arkansas?"

"That would be fabulous! I love that idea."

We decided that as soon as I got back from India, Mike would come to Oklahoma. Then together, we would plan our wedding.

Chapter Seventeen

FINDING A WAY HOME

ineteen of us left for India in early March 2020. However, we were delayed in Germany. Kendi told everyone, "My mom celebrated her birthday on three continents this year." She was correct. On my birthday, I was in the US, Europe and India.

The trip was packed with ministry. Arrows had opened so many doors for us that we had trouble meeting the demand. We were busy with the tour, not watching the news. At five o'clock in the morning one Friday, I received a text from my former secretary, Debbie Morris.

> Have you heard that they're closing the borders tonight at midnight? After midnight, no internationals can come into our country.

There had been a little chatter about COVID-19 before we left, But not a lot. I went straight to Jeff and Natalie's room and gave them the news. "I think we should get the whole team home as quickly as possible," I said, remembering my promise to Mike. "But I'm going home."

We didn't even have to consider what to do. We all agreed that we needed to get the team home. We canceled everything we had scheduled. The one thing we had in our favor was that India was 11½ hours ahead of Oklahoma.

One of the drawbacks however was that in India, no one is allowed inside an airport without a ticket. We woke the team and had them pack in a rush. Then, with our pastor friends Jackson and Moorthi along as interpreters, we headed straight for the airport.

Without a doubt, we needed a miracle. We needed airline tickets for 19 people. We needed to leave India and get into the United States before midnight.

Everyone was praying.

The heat in India is indescribable. Outside the airport, there was a large awning and chairs. We camped there while Jeff, Natalie and I worked on booking flights. Finally, leaving me with the dancers, Jeff, Natalie, Jackson and Moorthi drove across town to a travel agent.

There's no way to describe travel in India. It's beyond anything in our experience in the US. Trying to drive across the city is like running into dead end after dead end after dead end.

At first, the best they could do for us was get all 19 of us into Washington DC. From there, we'd have to rent three vans and drive. I wondered how any of us would be able to stay awake to drive after those flights.

Finally, they were able to get us booked...all the way into Oklahoma City. They made the harrowing trip across the city and back to the airport. They hadn't been back very long before getting a call from the travel agency. "You have to come back. Something wasn't signed."

Exhausted and unwilling to make that trip again, Natalie said, "I'm not going."

Jeff, Jackson and Moorthi made the exhausting trip again.

FAITH TO GET HOME

Meanwhile, I kept the dancers occupied by telling them the story of Mike and me. This was big news. Nobody knew it yet, and they wanted details.

Inside the airport, people in line to board flights were being pulled out if they coughed. They were also taking temperatures. We told everybody, "Whatever you do, do *not* cough!"

We finally got all 19 of us on the flight. Strange as it may seem, we were routed to the Middle East to go through customs. Since we had three internationals with us, Jeff had to do some talking. But somehow we managed to get everybody through.

The deadline for internationals entering the US was midnight.

We arrived at 10pm on Friday the 13th.

By now the whole country was starting to close.

Mike was already driving to Oklahoma the following week when my sister Fran said, "You guys had better get married now, before everything shuts down."

When he called from the road, I told him what Fran had said. "The courthouses are closing," Mike said. "Let's find out if we can get married."

I called the courthouse in Bentonville, Arkansas. It was closed. However, there were a few people still working inside. They agreed to send us our paperwork by email. They said we would fill it out and pull up in front of the courthouse. A masked person would come outside and take the paperwork. Then return with a marriage license.

Kendi had reached out to a Life Church pastor in Rogers, Arkansas, and asked him to perform the ceremony. The girls had also said that since they wouldn't be there, they wanted to send a photographer.

I called the pastor and the photographer to ask if they were available March 20. They both said the same thing. Nothing was going on, so they were available.

When Mike arrived in Oklahoma, he stayed with Kendi and her family March 18 and 19. On March 20, we left early to drive to Arkansas. We took our paperwork to the courthouse and everything went according to procedure. They brought us a marriage license. Afterwards, we drove 20 minutes to the chapel.

On the way, I called the chapel. "Is there someplace to change there?"

"Most people just book a hotel."

"That's not an option for us. They're all closed down."

"Come on. I'll help you with space here."

Then we were married!

We'd hoped to have our wedding meal at one of our favorite restaurants in Springdale, Arkansas: AQ Chicken. But it, like everything else, was closed. We finally found a Sonic who let us order a meal so long as we didn't get out of the car to eat it.

We were grateful.

Since there was literally no place open for our honeymoon, we drove back to my little house in Edmond. Throughout all this, Mike kept saying, "If you knew how much I loved you, you'd faint."

Just him saying it almost made me faint.

The next day, we went to Scotti's house. They had a sign to greet us.

Welcome Mr. & Mrs. Mike Sprouse.

Scotti, a fabulous cook, had ground wheat and made home-made bread for fresh, fabulous sandwiches.

Originally, we'd decided to keep both of our houses. However, as we talked about it on the way to Arizona to pick up Scout, we changed our minds. We decided to sell Mike's house.

When we arrived, we had to clean out his furniture and decide what to do with everything. My house was so tiny that there was no room for more. We found a realtor, moved all of his things into storage and then returned to Edmond with Scout. Our friends Ron and Phoebe Brown drove to Arizona and painted it.

His house sold in three days.

My house was darling, but it had two drawbacks. First and foremost, it had been a great house for me, but it wasn't *our* house. And it was too small for two people.

We started looking at houses. We finally found a lot over-looking a pond and a nature preserve. It had walking trails all through it. We bought the lot and starting building a new house in January, 2021. We moved in August of that same year.

I can't describe how wonderful my life is with Mike. We both love songs and often start singing the same song at the same time. Every day, we say the same thing at the same time. He whistles because he's happy. He sings. He finds fun places for us to visit and fun things to do all the time.

Mike is a healing balm to my soul.

He makes my heart sing.

THE WRONG ROAD

Looking back over my life, I realize that none of this would have happened to me if I hadn't had a revelation about the 10th chapter of John. I'd grown up in the church and lived more than 30 years of my life without knowing that I could hear God's voice. Then one day, I was challenged to take a fresh look at John 10.

That chapter took my breath away. Jesus calls us His sheep. He says that His sheep hear His voice and follow Him. He says, "No other voice will they follow."

I believe that John 10 is pivotal for anyone who wants to walk with God. We need to hear His voice. He's always talking. We just need to take the time to tune our ears to His frequency and listen. When I was a child, before I knew God's voice, I believed a lie that affected me for years until God set the record straight.

It happened after Mother died. Daddy lived the last two years of his life in a nursing home. It was a two-hour drive each way to see him. Visiting him was wonderful. Leaving him took an emotional toll on me every time.

May, Fran and I visited often. Our brother, Milton, lived in Seattle so he didn't get to visit much. Daddy's mind was playing tricks on him, and he seldom remembered our visits. However, he thought a man who worked in the nursing home was Milton. Daddy didn't remember our visits, but raved that Milton visited him every day.

I left the nursing home one day with my emotions in turmoil. As I drove past the Comanche Cemetery where Mother was buried, I decided to turn around and go back to visit her grave, which was easy to find. You drive into the cemetery, see a tree and there is her grave.

Except, on this day, I couldn't find it.

I couldn't even find the tree.

I was already emotional about leaving Daddy. Now I couldn't find Mother's grave. It was like being in the Twilight Zone. Nothing made sense and I felt almost hysterical, which was abnormal for me.

Then I realized that that there was more than one entrance to the cemetery. Mother's grave was accessed through the main entrance. Because I'd turned around to go back, I'd entered on the wrong road.

I started sobbing. "Father, what is this about?"

"When you took the wrong road, you couldn't find her grave. Years ago, you had a wrong thought. You thought your mother didn't love you. That

wrong road changed your viewpoint so that everything that happened after that confirmed your belief that she didn't love you.

"Your mother loved you. Always. She did the best she could. She'd been through a lot in her life and had a lot of wounds. She made mistakes, but she never had any ill intent toward you."

I realized that the enemy had tried to steal my identity the only way he has—through a lie. He planted the lie: *Your mother doesn't love you. Who loves you?*

I'd bought the lie and taken the wrong road in my thought life. It had taken me to a wrong belief that had a negative impact on my entire life up to that point.

I'm amazed that God cares about every detail of our lives— even our hurts and pains—for as long as we live. There's no expiration date on His love. He never says, "Well, you're too old now to be healed. Just live with it."

THE APOLOGY

One Sunday morning in January of 2019, I had a dream. Purple morning glories, pink periwinkles and red geraniums spilled over the sides of flowerpots and filled the flower beds with brilliant flashes of color in front of the farmhouse I grew up in outside of Corum, Oklahoma.

The house looked the age it had been when I grew up there. I looked the age I am now, and my granddaughter Charis stood beside me, at her current age. Together, we were watering the flowers.

A car drove up, and I watched in awe as my mother stepped out. She didn't look like she had the last time I'd seen her. She wasn't decimated by cancer. She appeared in her 40s.

She walked up to me and smiled in the morning sun. "Since the last time I saw you, I've wanted to apologize," she said.

I woke, blinking my eyes to see that I wasn't at the farm in Corum. I was at home in Edmond. I lay basking in the experience, caught somewhere between my life on the farm and this one.

Through that dream, God had healed the last remnant of my identity. Age, I understood, didn't matter much to God. Toddler or grandmother, it didn't matter. From the moment I lost my identity through my perception of Mother's rejection, God had been at work rebuilding what had been stolen from me.

He'd used school, music, the church and my relationship with Jesus. He'd filled a huge hole in my soul through Ken. To Ken, I was always his beloved. He considered me the most beautiful woman in any room. To him, I was the smartest, the prettiest and the kindest. Ken had never been stingy with his words. I heard how wonderful he believed me to be every day of our lives together.

Now Mike demonstrates how much he loves me every day of my life. He shows me through sending me romantic music. He tells me. He demonstrates his love by singing, by gifts, by flowers, by words and numerous acts of kindness.

None of that had been enough for God. He'd used my dream to heal decades-old hurts.

My mother apologized to me. Don't think she didn't.

It wasn't just a dream. We are spirit beings, and in the spirit my mother stepped out of that car and apologized to me. For some reason, the Lord let Charis witness the experience. I would ask Him about that later. However, it was interesting to me that in the dream I saw three generations. I saw Mother at age 40, I was my current age and Charis was 10.

The last piece of my heart had been put back together. God used love to tape and mud the walls back to their original state. He'd painted it the color of those red geraniums. The color of the Blood that had washed away the last remnants of pain.

Why?

Because He cares.

THE HEALER

It's that simple. You may not know that God cares that much about you. Since you received your first wounding here on earth, He has been healing, repairing and filling the holes in your soul.

He doesn't love me more than He loves you. It doesn't matter how old or how young you are. God is the Good Samaritan. He has taken you to an Inn where He pours oil and wine into your wounds.

He has tended you with care.

He has rejoiced over you with singing.

He knows that the traumas of life on earth made you forget who He created you to be.

You forgot to remember all the things that you knew before we came here.

You forgot that you are royalty.

You forgot that you are an heir together with Jesus.

He has given you a new name.

He is awakening you to His presence.

He's revealing your *true identity*.

He's reminding you that He has a plan for your life, and a purpose.

It's a plan for your good and not for your harm.

It's a plan to give you hope and a future.

He's revealing Himself to you.

You are His. You are beloved.

Pray this prayer:

Heavenly Father, please forgive me for all my sins. Thank you for paying the price for my sins through Jesus' death on the cross. Thank you for creating me. Thank you for a good plan for my life. Thank you for a good future and for hope. I ask Jesus to come into my heart. Lead me in your paths. Create in me my new identity. Help me to remember. In Jesus' name, I pray. Amen.

lifeinthefaithlane@yahoo.com

NOTES

11. A NEW WAY OF LIFE

1. How Much Sugar Do You Eat? https://www.dhhs.nh.gov/dphs/nhp/
documents/sugar.pdf
        accessed April 9, 2019

ABOUT THE AUTHORS

I met Melanie Hemry more than three decades ago. She came to an exercise class in our studio at Edmond Christian Academy. For years, I'd been reading her magnificent, inspiring writing in the *Believer's Voice of Victory* magazine. Each month when I received my magazine, I always read her story first. She had a wonderful way of making every story come to life and encouraging people to live a stronger more faith-filled life.

I was delighted to meet her, and over the years we became good friends.

To our joy, in the fall of 2012, Kenneth Copeland Ministries chose our story to be featured in the magazine. After hours of interviews, Ken and I had just one question. "Melanie, how on earth are you going to decide what to include in this story?"

"I'll lay it before the Lord," she told us. "He'll show me what part of your story needs to be told the most." Ken and I loved that answer. You can still read our story online in the March 2013 issue of the *Believer's Voice of Victory*.

Melanie's article ran in the magazine in March. Ken transitioned to heaven in August. After Ken went to heaven in 2013, Melanie and I became close buddies. We traveled together, talked together, prayed together, shared one another's challenges and victories, attended believer's conventions together and drew even closer to our King of kings. Although God brought an army of friends and relatives to help me during my seven years of being single, Melanie was my very close confidante, counselor and great friend.

Ken and I were 17 and 15 when we met. Our story was miraculous from the beginning. On our first date, he asked me to marry him. Neither of us ever changed our mind, or dated anyone else. We had an amazing 47 years together.

After his passing, I decided I would love to tell the world how faithful God has been in my life. Of course, I talked to Melanie about helping me. We even discussed telling it as a novel. However, we didn't want anyone to think the story wasn't factual. That's when we decided to write it as a memoir instead.

Several months prior to completing the manuscript for this book, God told me that I would remarry. That wasn't an idea I was comfortable with at first. Besides, I had no idea who I might marry. I considered stopping work on the book, since I knew my story was unfolding.

In January 2020, we had what we thought was a rough draft of the manuscript. Melanie had a copy on her computer. I had a copy on my computer. I also had a hard copy which I took with me on a Mercy Me cruise. I gave the hard copy to Bob Goff, asking him to read and endorse it.

Later, the strangest thing happened.

I couldn't find the copy on my computer.

Melanie couldn't find the copy on her computer.

Bob Goff had lost the hard copy.

Melanie and I both had brilliant IT guys search our computers. No one could recover the book.

We prayed in agreement that it would be restored. We expected it to show up any day. Weeks went by. Then months. Then years.

Three. Years.

By this time, Mike and I had been married for three years. I knew how it ended! However, it appeared that we would have to start over. The strange thing was that Melanie had been a writer for more than 30 years. In all that time, she'd never lost a manuscript. Everything she had was always backed up somewhere online.

One Sunday afternoon in early 2023, while Mike was watching a football game, Melanie and I went to a movie. On our way home she said, "I'd like to have you and Mike over for dinner one night this week. I also want to invite Andy Leong."

Andy was an amazing young man, who Mike and I wanted to know better. He was a pastor on staff at Church on the Rock, where Melanie attended. He was also the administrator for their Heartland Apostolic Prayer Network.

A few days later, we gathered at Melanie's house for dinner. I'd offered to bring a pecan pie, but she said no. Mike brought her flowers. She had made beef stroganoff, a family recipe of homemade braided bread which her Russian friends called Russian-American Friendship Bread, salad and apple pie.

While the bread was baking, Melanie said, "Bea, I forgot to give you your Christmas present." I was surprised because we don't usually exchange Christmas presents, and this was well after Christmas.

She brought me a beautifully wrapped present. It had tissue paper with bees and beehives on it. That was special to me, but nothing could have prepared me for what was inside the bag.

It was the printed manuscript of this book.

I was speechless. Then I said, "How did you find this?"

Melanie pointed at Andy. How Andy found the book is above my paygrade. I'll let him tell that part of the story.

> "Even though I work fulltime for the church as a pastor, worship leader and administrator," Andy explains, "my degree is actually in computer science. One day Melanie stopped by the church and stepped into my office to visit. She asked some technical questions. I started to answer her, but I decided to find out why she wanted to know.
>
> "She told me that Bea's book had disappeared from her computer. I told her I would come by after work. She said not to bother. She'd already had two IT guys check her entire computer. I asked why she hadn't told me about the problem before. She said she knew how busy I was and that she didn't want to bother me.
>
> "The man who had taken care of her IT problems for years had passed away. I asked how she was backing up her documents up now. She told me about the online services she used. I told her that I had all the church computers backed up on external hard drives and Dropbox. I also insisted that I would come by after work.

"When I arrived at her office later that day, Melanie told me she'd been thinking about what I said. She explained that when Ron was alive, he had her computer backed up on an external hard drive. If she could find that, she was sure to find the book. She also said that Ron had her documents backed up on Dropbox.

"I sat down at her computer and searched for her Dropbox account. Within 10 minutes, I had found the account, accessed it and found your book."

That's how this book came to be in your hands. I believe that God hid it until my story was finished. Melanie and I have had great fun adding all that's happened in the past three years. I pray that you have as much fun reading it.

Bea Sprouse

Made in USA - North Chelmsford, MA
1381841_9798852074836
08.28.2023 1007